AN
ACT
OF
WOMAN
POWER

AN
ACT
OF
WOMAN
POWER

Kisma K. Stepanich

1469 Morstein Road
West Chester, Pennsylvania 19380 USA

An Act of Woman Power
by Kisma K. Stepanich

Library of Congress Card Number: 89-50768
International Standard Book Number: 0-914918-93-1

Manufactured in the United States of America

Published by Whitford Press,
A division of
Schiffer Publishing, Ltd.
1469 Morstein Road
West Chester, Pennsylvania 19380
Please write for a free catalog.
This book may be purchased from the publisher.
Please include $2.00 postage.
Try your bookstore first.

*This book is dedicated
to my Mother, Betty,
and to all Goddesses who walk this land.*

With warmth and love
I would like to thank Sweet Lisa,
whose hard work helped make this book a reality,
and
to my special companion,
Kevin,
whose "adventurer" took me into the wilderness.

CONTENTS

PART ONE

Women Who Bleed for Life

PART ONE

WOMEN WHO BLEED FOR LIFE

Sisters of the Moon
We gather once more
To celebrate the bloom
of love and light
and Mother Earth[1]

...The new moon was appearing in Aquarius. Winter held us within its center. For the first time in days the evening sun shone with rose and purple as it settled below the horizon, washing the earth in grey twilight.

Four women arrived at my door. Each found and read the note attached to the outside of the front door:

"Greetings Loved One-

"Tonight is a time of stillness. Please remain silent. Tonight we celebrate with reverence. Flow with the ceremony and there will be no need for questions.

"Please prepare yourself now for ritual by using bedroom or bathroom. When you return you will be handed a taro card. Please study this card and keep it with you for ritual and meditation.

"There will be a few times where I will guide you with words, please, remain quiet. The evening chant: "Special One".

"You may enter now. Peace."

All was quiet. The four women stood wide-eyed at the side of the living room. In the center where I stood was an altar. I lit a white work candle and motioned to the woman nearest the light switch to flip it off.

The room went dark, and slowly the bold single flame of the work candle eased the atmosphere with flickering light.

I stood in front of the altar facing north. I looked down into the crystal, resting in the center of the altar, waiting for a sign to begin. The crystal caught the light of the single flame and flared brilliant color. I sighed. I picked up my athame. In both hands I held it heart level in front of me and closed my eyes.

Gradually, my breathing became steady. I followed the breath in and out, flowing with the natural rhythm of life; connecting with the one thing we are very sure of and never have to stop to think about - the breath. We inhale, we exhale. It is constant. It is natural. It is a basic part of our physical make-up. We know that as long as we breath we are alive. So, I followed the breath into my aliveness and settled peacefully in my center.

Inhale, exhale...inhale, exhale...inhale, exhale. Steady, calm...steady, calm...steady, calm. The tension of the physical limitations of the body ease. The wild racing of the mind slows. The throbbing of the heart beats steadily. All levels of being begin to shift into a new mellowness, and blend. All the energy centers relax and align. Slowly, the ethereal body fills with balanced energy, and glows. A sense of awareness lightens, and the lips cannot help but round at the corners into a beautiful, peaceful smile. Once more we become our spirit.

I opened my eyes and watched the stillness of the work candle. Yes, the energy in the room had become grounded. I would cast a formal circle tonight, I thought to myself as I laid the athame down. I knelt before the altar and gazed into the crystal. I felt the shifting of the four women behind me as they knelt down where they stood.

Reaching out I took the work candle and lit the two, blue altar candles. The room became brighter. The flames were steady. I picked the athame up and held it out in front of me. With a deep, full breath I turned the blade down and lowered it into a platter of earth. "I call earth to bind my spell." Raising the knife above my head I traced the luminscate in the air. "Air to speed its travel well." The tip was lowered into the right candle flame. "Bright as fire shall it glow." A second time I pointed the tip down and lowered it into a chalice of pure water. "Deep as the water shall it flow." Grasping the handle with both hands, blade pointed up, I held the athame at full arms length out in front of me over the altar. "Count the elements four-fold. In the fifth the spell shall hold."[2] *I brought the blade to my lips and kissed it, blowing the breath of my spirit on it. "So mote it be." I held the knife to my heart.*

Rising I moved to the east quarter of the circle, and there pointed the tip of the athame to the east. Grounding the energy I moved round the circle carving a boundary in the air, marking the perimeter of sacred space. Starting east, moving south, west, north and closing east, I focused my attention on the fine blue light of energy emanating from the end of the blade.

Returning to center I laid the athame down and picked up the chalice of pure water in my left hand. Raising it above my head I blessed it. With my right hand I picked up a bowl of salt and raised it above my head.

"Blessed be, oh element of water. Blessed be, oh element of earth. Salt and water be cleansed. Cast out all impurities. Take in all that is healing and pure. By the power of the Mother and Her lover. So mote it be."

With both containers in place on the altar, I knelt before it, and picked up the athame placing the tip down into the salt.

"Blessed be art of magick." With the tip I scooped up salt and placed it in the chalice of water. The alchemical transformation of elemental blending was enacted. The art of magick; the chemical reaction of elements, the combining of forces of elements to create and manifest into the physical.

With the blade I swirled the water and salt to the right three times blending the elements into oneness. "May these tools, and this altar be cleansed." With the athame raised over the altar the water gently dripped off the blade and fell on the tools and the altar. The athame was laid to rest.

Cupping both hands around the chalice I raised it full arms length in front of me, level with my heart. "Inner and outer, body and soul, be cleansed."

Closing my eyes, I focused within. The energy of purity and healing stirred and shot down the two arms stretched before me. They were stiff with energy and felt strong as stone. The Priestess of Ishtar was surrounding my body and the force of her existence took over. I surrendered to her will, and opened my eyes to watch as if from a distance.

The mixture in the chalice had become potent. Whisps of white cloud rose above the lip of the cup. The arms brought the chalice into the body and cradled it close to the heart. The beating of the heart could be heard as it mingled with the pure essence of the chalice. It thundered through my mind.

I could feel the nurturing love of the Priestess pouring out from her center, and flooding into the center of the chalice. Slowly, she raised the chalice to her lips and blew her life force upon the surface.

"Let all who seek to enter the sacred circle be purified," Her deep voice, heavy with energy, spoke. The bitter, yet refreshing liquid, ran down my throat. Turning to look at the four women still kneeling at the side of the room my arm held the chalice out to them. Slowly, a red haired woman stood and walked forward. Carefully, she accepted the chalice in her hands and raised it to her lips to drink the elixir. The Priestess raised her right hand. With two fingers she touched the center of the woman's brow and sent "awakening" to her consciousness. With the same hand she took back the chalice and leaned forward kissing the woman on the lips welcoming her in the circle, while sealing her purification with blessings of love. In turn each woman came forward and went through the same process.

As the last women finished, the Priestess took the chalice and walked to the east. There she lit the east candle and moved south espurging the sacred boundary with the water purifying the space. She moved ritualistically round the circle until she came full circle.

Returning the chalice to the altar she lit a bundle of herbs on fire and placed them in a clay dish. Turning she retraced her steps to the east quarter. She held the smudge pot up to the ceiling, then lowered it down in a straight line sealing off the first of six gateways. To the south she performed the same act. West, north, the same, then returned to the east completing the circle. She moved to the center and held the pot up to the heavens moving it in a clock-wise circle. Lowering it to the earth she moved the pot in a counter-clock-wise circle, then returned the pot to the altar.

The circle had been established. All who stood within had been cleansed and blessed. Silently, the Priestess moved once again to the east quarter. Bowing her head she raised her hands, pressed together, to her lips. All was quiet. She closed her eyes, and opened her mind to the spirit of east.

East power opened its gateway with a yellow light illuminating the doorway into the mind. The lightness of the element rose like the morning sun, and brightened reality. The soul took flight in the brightness soaring high, high above the mind into the cavatives of consciousness.

It is at this height the clarity of mind peers down on everything and sees that there are no limitations. Suddenly, inspiration shoots through the veins, awakening the intellect, and freedom flows through every cell.

The Priestess could feel the air move through her hair and began moving her head from side to side. Instinctually her body began to move tracing the luminscate with the flowing garment on her body. High and light the "a" vowel sound began to flow from her throat. She moved swiftly like a bird, and freely like the air. High in consciousness she danced with the spirit of the eastern watchtower, and found friendship with the energy and power of air. As she lowered back into her body she brought with her the essence of air. The energy was awakened and formed a protective sphere around its gateway of the circle. Opening her eyes she smiled as the flash of east settled into the reality of her dimension.

She moved to the south. Again she raised her hands in prayer attitude, lowered her head. All was quiet. She closed her eyes, opened her soul to the spirit of south.

South power opened its fiery gateway racing forth its flaming fingers into the soul. The intensity of the element flared like the mid-day sun and flood-lit reality. The red blood soared through the veins opening every vessel with passion.

It is in the south that the hunger of the soul jumps up, and the ferocious energy leaps out touching every direction. The spirit becomes uncontainable, absorbed in this innocence of desire. There is nothing to stop its dance as it becomes wild in ecstasy. Pure and wild. It sparks creation. It gives the energy to fulfill.

The Priestess could feel the fire coursing through her veins, igniting every inch of her being. Instantly her hands shot up over her head forming a triangle with her fingers. Her body shimmied with erotic passion. Wild and crackly the sound of the vowel "e" rose from her throat. Engulfing the space, her frenzied body cast shadows against the wall. The shadows of a large flame reaching and yearning for life.

As she rose with the flame she understood the quickening pulse of the wild animal as it sprints after its prey. She felt the exploding release of passion and the bursting spark of creation. As she raced with the blood in her veins she danced with the spirit of fire, and found understanding with the energy and power of the south. As the flame within her stilled and brought her back within her body she held the essence of the south.

Opening her eyes the wall of flame stood defiantly around its quarter of circle, protecting the gateway. Sweat ran down her body; the wetness carried her to the west. There she closed her eyes, lowered her head to meet her poised hands.

Instantly, the crashing of waves could be heard as she faced the keeper of the west watchtower. Her breathing matched the rhythm of the tide; incoming, outgoing...incoming, outgoing...incoming, outgoing. Bluish-black twilight surrounded her, and there, spreading out before her was a still pool of water. The depth of the pool was endless, and the blackness of its depth naturally drew her eye to the center. Within the center a sliver of silver-white light began to glow. The new moon shone. The water lightly rippled with the pull of moon on tides. Calmness of the water began to reflect the image of the Priestess, and there, the releasing of emotions poured forth from her face.

The stillness of the water reflects the emotional body, showing us the true side of spirit. One cannot hide from this reflection, for it is the mirror of our heart and rests eternally within us. Once we dare to gaze upon the waters of the heart and feel all the emotions which swim deep within the waters of the pool, we find we can calmly float upon the surface of the water, and eventually, the tide will gently bring us to the edge once more.

The water within the Priestess' body tugged at her. Automatically her hands lowered to hold her womb chakra. Slowly, rhythmically, her pelvis began to rock back and forth. As ripples of intuition flowed up from her second chakra her body naturally followed. Her knees bent slightly and her hips made a circling motion. As the spirit of water rose within her body her hands rose to her heart, and there, her whole body, including her head, rolled and moved in circles dancing with the west.

As she merged with the power of water she realized and accepted the waning of life; the surrendering of one's ego to the darkness of the spirit. For the journey through the darkness of death brings forth the true power, the true essence of life; the combining of the three greatest truths: knowledge, wisdom and love.

As the pool of water slowly faded and her body stilled, the Priestess knew fear of darkness was ignorance. And as that wisdom flooded her heart she opened her eyes. The surging of water flowed around the west watchtower forming its protective pool around this quarter of the circle.

With her mental, emotional and spiritual bodies awakened, the Priestess approached the last gateway. There in the north she stopped and resumed her position of humbleness.

All was still as she stood in front of the north watchtower. She heard the rumbling of earth before she felt it shake and split open. She fell deep within the crevice and continued to fall deeper and deeper into the earth. At first, after she came to a stop on a granite shelf, she felt claustrophobic from the earth surrounding her. The gasses of sulphur clogged her throat and she couldn't breath. Then once more the ground gave out from underneath her and she slide down an opening much like the mouth of a cave coming to rest in a large cavity filled with mineral pools of water, gasses waifing in the air, flashes of fire spurting up around molten lava in its center.

It was hot and humid. Rich and powerful. With each breath she felt the essence of the earth's minerals pour into her body saturating every inch of her. She grew strong and mighty. She felt powerful. She had arrived, at last, on the threshold of the physical body itself.

Here was substance, solidness. The composition of all the elements coming together. The foundation of which life itself needs to live off of. Here, was the center of reality of life on planet earth. Here, was the body of our great Mother. Here, was the beginning of our own physical existence.

The Priestess felt the support of the earth. She felt the strength of her own body and wanted to combine the two. Her legs began pounding into the earth. Stomping and driving the palms of her hands down toward the ground. The sound of the "u" vowel growled deep in her body. She rocked with the spirit of earth and connected deeply with the energy of the earth. "Powerful, powerful, powerful," beat in her heart. The watchtower of the north grew tall and broad as a mountain. As she continued to ground the energy she was brought back into her body. Trembling, she opened her eyes and saw the sheer cliff of granite surrounding the northern quarter. Its protection was inpenetrable. She stood a moment longer, feeling the crystalization of her own strength.

Stoically she walked round to the east closing the circle. There she bowed and turned to face the mesmerized women standing in the center. The expressions on their faces showed the Priestess that they, too, had experienced the energies she invoked. Now, she would take them all the way. Now, she would bring forth the true essence of their energy – the Goddess.

Taking hold of two women's hands the rest automatically formed a circle. She closed her eyes knowing they would do the same. Gently they began to sway left to right to left to right. Their breaths unified becoming one. Their hearts beat as one. The energy running through their clasped

1

8 *An Act of Woman Power*

hands connecting, merging, and becoming one. The Priestess opened the oneness to the Goddess.

As the residue of each of the four quarters connected, the small circle of women became the combined components of life. The center of their circle began to glow with the flowing energy of their light centers. The pillars of their bodies became cemented in the ground, and the spirit of their life drew up expanding, filling their awareness with a sense of greatness beyond anything they had ever known.

The pulsing of the heart center blew open, and the center of the circle was flooded with pure light. The blood in their veins began to heat, escalating their breath. The life force within them began to shift and elevate their consciousness, opening them, bringing together the nature of their unity, merging the female energy. Brightly, magnificently the Goddess rose up, and spreading out Her arms gathered the circle to Her bosom.

The Priestess felt the Goddess take control. She surrendered the oneness to this great energy. Quietly, but urgently "ma-ma" escaped her lips.

Soon, the complete circle was one voice singing the sound of creation. "Ma-ma", rose through the center of the circle, spiraled up and out into the world of energy.

The fullness of each woman was realized. Each woman was feeling, completely, the very core of her existence, of her own energy. And in doing so connected with the invisible cord, which connects all women to their signature.

Slowly, the singing quieted. The Goddess filled each heart with existence and quietly faded into the back of consciousness while continuing to flow passively through the center of their bodies.

The women continued to sway back and forth until even that small, nurturing movement came to a stop. There they stood. Quiet. Still. Each a part of a whole.

The Priestess gently gathered them into a group hug. Eyes opened and gazed into eyes. Soft smiles danced on the lips. Love surrounded them.

In its own time, the small circle released its oneness. Each women found a comfortable spot on the ground. The Priestess gave them a few minutes to relax before leading them into a guided meditation.

Signaling the women to relax and close their eyes, the Priestess switched on a tape deck. Soft music began to fill the room. Her words cemented the experience they had just gone through.

"I listen to the voice of the universe as it speaks within me. It is the voice of truth and it guides me unerringly along the paths of my life. Somewhere deep within me, in the perfect bud of my soul, there stands an immobile universe where all things and all law lie revealed. I reach within to this place of peace and quietness. I harken to the voice of my heart. I close my eyes and sense a living, breathing universe dwelling within me, and I dwelling in it. I am one with all people and all life and all things. I move in accordance with divine law. All the limitless power of creation is mine to draw upon, for it is in me and one with me and I am a part of it. The answer comes with the question; the path is lighted with the first step; the way is cleared with the looking; the goal is in sight with the desire. I know that I am fulfilling the fondest wish of Goddess for I place myself in Her hands, taking each step of my life boldly and strongly, for it is Goddess who prompts me, and Goddess moves with sureness. I see tomorrow for I know today, and this day is Mother of tomorrow. The things of my life are the children of my thoughts, and my thoughts of today are even now bearing the child of tomorrow. All that is good I desire; all that is evil I refuse to accept. By attaining, I do not deprive. All that is and ever will be is available to every woman; she need only ask and it shall be given. I bind myself to the power for good that surges heavenward all around me. The limits and inhibitions of my past are gone. Each day is a new birth of my soul. Each day is another step on my journey to a oneness with Goddess. I do not seek, I know. I do not strive, I am guided."[3]

As the music ended the Priestess began the evening chant bringing each woman out of the meditation.

"There is a special one inside. All the stars and all the galaxies, run through her hands like beads."[4]

Soon, all the women were singing. Slowly, the song was turned inward, becoming a hymn to the Goddess of each woman. So personal did it become that tears slid silently down their faces. The chant quietly ended.

Blessings of cakes and wine was performed in silence. The Priestess held the platter of cakes over the center of the altar and each woman placed her hands just above the cakes, forming a matrix of fingers. With bowed heads and closed eyes they sent forth personal blessings. The same was done with the chalice of wine.

The two containers were passed around while each woman took a cake *and sip of wine. The wine continued to be passed until the chalice was empty.*

The Circle Book was also passed so each woman could write down her thoughts. Giggling broke out in the circle, as did pantomiming. The women were drunk on their own energy and the sweetness of the cakes helped lighten the atmosphere.

When everyone was finished writing in the Circle Book, and cakes and wine were finished, the Priestess stood before them. Silently she thanked the Goddess, and bid each of the elements farewell.

Gathering the women to the center, joining hands once more, she opened circle; ending the rite. Exclamations of laughter, and amazement rang through the room as the women hugged and kissed, and found places to sit.

I walked over and flipped the light switch on. I was dizzy and my energy was spent, but the women wanted to share their feelings, I was more than willing to oblige them.

"In the silence I heard my mind laughing with joy and happiness. I felt as if I would burst forth in the silence like a star child." Jenny, with long red hair, was the first to speak.

"It was like, well, in the still center was the spinning universe; a Lady dancing. It was very serious for me, because I felt as if a seed was awakening. A seed awakening the silence which holds all truths. I mean, we very seldom take the time to listen to the wordlessness. Especially, not in ceremony." Georgia was a vivacious court reporter who always was quick to speak; often interrupting circle with a good joke.

"Well," Teresa, a heavy set blonde hesitantly started speaking, stopped, then fingered her wedding ring.

She looked up at me and smiled, I understood immediately. The experience had been her break-through. Teresa had finally experienced what we had been working with for the last three months.

"Well," she continued. "In the stillness I felt as if I was somber grass. Yet, within there was mirth, and without the faintest hint of laughter. Moving and dancing into an almost frenzic exuberance. As we welcomed the Goddess, for the first time, I felt we touched heart with an explosive energy. I was overwhelmed. I still am."

All the women nodded in agreement. Linda was the last to speak. She had been searching the longest for a sense of identity. I had given her the simple truth of looking within, instead of out. And in the year I had known her she was beginning to shift her focus and see her own transformation taking place. With a huge smile she looked at me.

"Woman, seed, embryo, birth, salmon, bird, seed, rebirth, comedy, life," she exploded. Her eyes twinkled. We all started laughing. It had been a fantastic ceremony.

We all sat quietly for a moment. Eventually, their eyes turned towards me, waiting for my rendition of the evening.

"In the stillness we came to the last new moon of the season of the waning. Now we stand ready to bloom with the spring."

I paused to let this sink in.

"Tonight, for the first time, we actually accomplished something very powerful. Very spiritual. We became one, and the female energy rose up out of our oneness and embraced us."

Smiles spread across their faces as they looked from one to the other then back to me.

"You have shown a willingness to open to each other. Of lowering all your walls, of stripping down to nakedness in front of each other. Your spirit has over-taken you and spoken. Your spirit has actively told you, 'you are ready to discover your own power; the common bond between women; the life blood; the ancient mystery of life.'"

Linda clapped at this. "I am ready Kisma." She spoke boldly. The other three nodded murmuring in agreement. I looked each one in the eye.

"Good. We'll move forward into deeper water. For now, take home your awareness from this night. Write about it, work with it, remember it. Do not let it die the minute you walk out of here. Try to keep that female energy with you. Focus. Concentrate."

I stood. "I love you all, but I'm tired." I smiled as they understood what I was saying and began gathering their belongings to leave.

"See you next week." I called after them as the sound of their feet on the stairs faded, and I stood alone on the porch, looking up to the starry winter sky...

CHAPTER I

THE MOON

The pull of moon on tides. A simple truth we grow up hearing, and yet, take for granted. As women, this statement has more meaning than we realize.

The first lesson for women should always be our connection with the moon. The moon our guiding light, our calendar.

The Lunar Cycle

Each year we travel round an imaginary wheel consisting of 13 lunar cycles. It is a wheel based upon nature; the basic nature of the earth and the heavens, and not of human kind.

One lunar cycle consists of 28 to 28 1/2 days; which is the amount of time it takes the moon to complete its 360 degree revolution about the earth. Since our modern calendar consists of 365 days it takes 13 lunar cycles plus one day to match it. (This is where the old phrase "a year and a day" comes from).

The lunar cycle of 28 days is broken up into five phases (three major and two minor), beginning with: 1) the new, or crescent moon, 2) the waxing phase, 3) the full moon, 4) the waning phase, 5) and the dark moon (when no part of the moon is visible in the night sky).

The new, or crescent moon, is seen approximately 2 to 4 days after the dark moon (depending on the season). The waxing (increasing) moon phase takes approximately 10 days to reach the position where we see a full moon. The full moon is round for three days. The waning (decreasing) moon phase takes approximately 10 days to reach the position where we no longer see any trace of the moon, thus taking us into the dark moon. The dark moon lasts about three days (again depending on the season).

Since the moon is visible only at night, the 24 hour cycle (which we call one day) begins when the sun sets.[5]

The New Crescent Moon

The silver sliver appears in the evening sky. The new moon. The re-birthing of light at night. The lunar cycle is beginning its process once again.

We have come to know that the new moon is the time for planting "seeds" in our lives. The seeds of the mind, of emotion, or of physical desires. The mood/attitude we hold at new moon will influence us for the balance of that particular lunar cycle.

We know that whatever seeds planted with the new moon they will grow as the moon waxes, and become manifested in our lives as the fullness of the moon appears in the sky.

At new moon the woman's body should be slender. She stands as a virgin. The womb is void of blood, and water retention is at its lowest. Physical energy is re-birthing, and emotions are re-balancing.

As women, we find we are more quick witted at this time. We turn our mind towards finances, healing, love, and become protective of physical objects in our space.

We feel young and alive. We go out and socialize. We laugh, and tease, and play. When angered, we allow the energy to flare, but find forgiveness comes easier at this time.

As the moon waxes so does our energy. We actualize some of the goals we have set for ourselves. We begin new projects, and finish old ones. We study and experiment.

This is the busy time for us. Plants get tended, floors swept, new pillows for the couch made. Beautify and enhance. Self-actualize. Self-empower.

Full Moon

Kue bella luna! The beautiful, full moon rises in the night. Round and full she travels across the night sky illuminating the darkness, and mirroring back the emotions deep within our hearts.

The seeds that were planted with the energy of the new moon are brought to fruition. Long term goals are looked at; the changes which have taken place realized. We seem to find our intuition heightened and showing us a clear path ahead.

Our bodies should be full and swollen at this time. The tide is in, and our bodies are filling with water preparing for life. We are fertile, and ovulate. Our emotions and intuitions are at peak.

We are filled with the essence of our womanhood. The full moon represents the swollen belly heavy with child. Our energies are extremely lascivious. We look up at the moon and smile. We dance in her light. We are wild and uncontainable. We rejoice.

All our energy is peaking with one full climax.

...The full moon shone in the night. Gail and Lisa arrived. They were excited. Together the three of us had been working so hard on controlling our own bodies. We were ready to celebrate.

Quickly, they changed into their gowns while I finished setting up the altar. As they returned to the living room, I instructed them to sit and relax a moment while sipping red raspberry tea allowing their energy to quiet down. I lit sage and carried it around the room in a circle cleaning the space. I had them both stand, saged them, then finished with myself.

I picked up the darbuka drum instructing them to ground and center in their own way as I played the drum. I told them that the tempo of the drumming would change as a sign to move onto the next step of the process.

"Closing your eyes focus on your breath. Follow it to your heart. As you exhale release your contact with the outside world." I watched them breath for a few seconds, then joined in with the drumming.

I closed my own eyes and followed my breath to my heart. As my breath grew steady I focused on the base of my spine. There the glowing of energy began to rise and continued to swirl until it was traveling up my spine in an ascending spiral. As it reached the crown of my body a second flowing of energy sprang forth in a descending spiral ending at the base.

I breathed with the duality of the two currents, and felt my own kundalini energy merge.

Roots of energy light sprang out from my base and dove down into the earth. The roots pushed through the top soil past the granite layers. They dove deeper spreading out through the layers of rich minerals and moisture until, at last, they struck the molten core of the Mother.

Here my roots plunged into the very center of the core, and with each breath I drew up the powerful, rich, supportive energy of Mother Earth. As this solid energy entered my base it surged through each of my centers, filling every inch of my being with strength. The Mother and I were one energy.

As I released my breath the connection was cemented. Almost immediately branches of energy sprang forth from my crown chakra and began climbing, reaching up towards the heavens.

The rhythm of the drum had shifted. With each "dum" my branches lifted higher and higher into the heavens. All the light of life reflected there. Sun light, star light, planet light flowed everywhere. When it seemed my branches could go no further there appeared a core of light and the tips of the branches reached forward surging up into the very center of this brilliant light.

I felt the universe flooding down into my crown, illuminating every particle of my being.

Suddenly, I was a conduit of energies, the rich heavy energy of the earth, the bright, airy energy of the heavens. Both flowed through me.

As I exhaled, the connection with the universe was intact. I drew in my breath again, and the two energies rushed into my center exploding into a blissful merging of existence.

The drumming grew faster. I opened to the duality of the energies as they filled and saturated my being. I joined my energy to the two, and the three became one.

The drumming was a powerful beat. "Dum, dum, dum," it repeated over and over again in the space around us. Then softly it altered and lulled all the energies into a spiral spinning round and round the circle, until each of our energies hooked up. The three of us became linked together as one.

Softly, the drumming stilled. Only our breath could be heard as it milked *the sudden silence.*

We opened our eyes, looked at each other, then laughed. A powerful connection had been established right from the start.

I called in the quarters. Together we chanted the Charge of the Star Goddess. We smoked the pipe.

No one quite knows what happened, but the next thing we knew all three of us were up and dancing moon-wise in the circle. I began drumming, Gail clacked the singing sticks and Lisa shook the rattles. Our voices reached up to the moon.

> *"Come children, come and dance,*
> *Earth, wind, fire and sea.*
> *Come join the dance of life*
> *Earth, wind, fire and sea."[6]*

It became a chorus of angel voices lifting to the heavens. Our voices rang out to all the open souls living within a 25 mile radius from where we danced. We seduced, innocently, our star brothers, and the universe poured down its very sweet and tender love.

We slowed, turning to the center. The drum continued to beat, but shifted into a new rhythm. Each of us could feel a shifting take place. The doorway was opening.

The "I Am" chant rose from our throats. Our spirits singing. Our energy elevated. We entered the door.

> *"I am the soul,*
> *I am the light divine,*
> *I am love,*
> *I am will,*
> *I am fixed design,*
> *I am the Goddess.*
>
> *"I open to my higher self.*
> *I open to my unfoldment.*
> *I totally open myself to the One.*
> *I am Gaia."[7]*

As the last vibration from both the drum and our voices carried out of the room and flowed to the world around us, we smiled, and looked deep in each other's eyes. We had crossed over.

Instinctively we began to move. Our instruments joined in. We danced our celebration of life. We played our celebration of the moon. We toned and sang out affirmations, celebrating ourselves.

It became an intensely personal moment. Each caught within our own dance. The circle filled with swirling masses of energy. It seemed as if everywhere I looked I could see the outline of the whirling dervishes as they spiraled in ecstasy; celebrating in their oneness with Allah.

As I circled round the altar my eyes were brought to the center of the flame of the candle. I found myself coming to a stop. There I stood immersed in the glowing redness and the blue flame contained within.

Laying our instruments down we joined hands recentering. Closing our eyes we breathed. "Ma-ma," rang out. Again a beautiful chorus of spirit vibrated out, the vibration blending to an end. We stood still, locked in the middle of the spirit.

From the waist down our bodies became cement pillars. A reinforcing matrix of energy dove down into the earth. We were solid. Our foundation established.

Our strength expanded, engulfing us within an invisible force field of support. Suddenly, I received a great dose of shakti (Mother energy), and momentarily, from my waist up, I lost balance and began to sway backwards. The support was there immediately though, and within seconds I was standing straight and secure.

I felt our crowns release and the spirit of each grow ten feet tall. I looked down upon our circle.

My announcement on earth was made by the celestial beings as I was kissed by all the spirits present.

"Feel the power," they whispered to me.

"Feel your strength. Know that you are this power. All mysteries live within you. For you are a mystery. But we are not mysteries to ourselves. We know ourselves. We know our power, our sacredness. We know our life. But life itself is a mystery. You are that mystery."

I stood surrounded by the echoing of their voices. Everything made sense at that moment. There were no mysteries, of course. The only mystery comes from the mind of mankind. We make the mysteries, because we are the biggest mystery of all. We are life.

I could feel Lisa and Gail coming back into their bodies. I squeezed hold of their hands and let go my grasp. When I opened my eyes I saw the faces of two angels standing before me.

I shared my message with them. Lisa said her message had been to stop holding back in her throat center, that the Goddess' voice wanted to flow. Gail needed to stop clinging to self, to release: there was no need to be timid. She needed to become her Goddess.

We laughed at the truth of each message. We felt giddy, and not quite back. So, we decided to sing our Tribe song five times.

It was funny, at first, we were so scattered and could barely remember the words. We giggled through the first round. But as each round passed our voice grew strong. The fifth time we sang clearly with conviction.

I thanked the Goddess, life, the father, the universe, and the spirit. I dismissed the quarters, opening circle, ending the rite.

A vortex had been achieved. A true bond connected. Shifting had been experienced and I was being allowed to become. Soon, Lisa and Gail would be shifting on their own. A major accomplishment had taken place this night. A year of lessons and hard work had paid off. I applauded the ladies...

The Dark Moon

The night sky is dark. Nowhere, is there any sight of the moon. The world is covered in total blackness. This is the time that ghost stories are told round a camp fire. This is the time small children cry out in the night from bad dreams.

This is the time of darkness.

Of our own inner darkness. Energy has turned inward, traveling down the pathways of our own shadow. We are retrospective. We are recluse.

We have come to know that this is the time for banishing evil from our lives. Releasing negative emotions. Examining the big MO (modus operandi) of our actions.

The full moon has passed. Woman's body is still full and swollen. If there was no conception of man's life seed, her womb releases the blood, and it begins to weep.

Our hormones are changing. Our physical body is changing. Our emotions are extremely sensitive. We want nothing more than to curl up on the couch with a good book, or soak in the bathtub, and be left alone.

We find excuses not to go out, or attend social gatherings.

Our psychic is so "right on", that if someone does not really like us we pick up on it. If someone has a hidden agenda we feel manipulated, becoming grouchy. We know. We just know, for some unexplained reason, that so-and-so just doesn't like us, or is angry with us. Woman's intuition reaches new heights at this time.

So, we must focus on ourselves, dare to go within, and walk the dark corridor. Come face-to-face with the black mirror and gaze upon it until, within the darkness, we see the stirrings of light shine through, illuminating the black edges.

So often in the midst of the darkness lies all our hidden power. We are so afraid to claim our power that it has become a villain surrounded by the black cape.

Throw back the hood of that black cape. See the face that smiles back. The beautiful raw and wild woman who dwells hidden, deep inside your darkness. The woman, behind all your intense emotions. The woman, behind all your action.

Surprisingly enough, you will find a queen. A strong, powerful, yet beautiful queen.

The Shadow Queen Visualization

(Note:*= pause a heartbeat or two; **= pause a minute or two; ***= allow ten minutes of silence.)

It is important to find the time and place where you will not be interrupted, and will be able to perform the following journey in solitude.

It is best to perform this journey with another person, but if you have not found other women to work with, then make a recording so you will get the maximum benefit of it. Remember, this is a scary journey to make, because you are willingly going into your shadow. The shadow is the side of us we are afraid to face, because we are afraid we will not like what we see.

Give yourself permission to feel these emotions, and know that you will return from this journey a new woman. Upon returning you will begin to understand that the shadow which dwells within our hearts, is simply a side of our spirit that has never been birthed. As a woman willing to come face-to-face with her shadow, you will give birth to your own feminine energy – the Shadow Queen!

Relax, and begin by breathing naturally and fully. Follow your breath in and out, until you feel a calmness spreading through your body as well as your mind.*

Follow your next breath into what feels, or seems like your center, wherever that may be within your body. Know that your center is a safe space for you to go to when you begin a journey, such as this one.*

As you dwell within your center you will find all fear diminishing. A peace will come over you. Relax here for just a moment.*

Visualize an opening within your center. This opening is very dark. You turn to face it, and with each breath you find yourself floating through the opening, and travelling deeper and deeper within your consciousness.

You are comfortable, and floating deeper and deeper.

There is darkness surrounding you, but you are not afraid. You float deeper and deeper within the essence of your being.

Naturally, and peacefully you find you have come to a solidness beneath you. Your awareness is resting upon this solidness. You have traveled deep within the very center of your darkness.

As you stand within this darkness you see shapes and images begin to materialize before you. They are moving around and around you. Some of them are fears, anger, hate, sides of your personality which you equate with negativity.

It is okay to allow these negative images to appear before you. Know that they are part of you, and there is no need to reject them. Stand there and simply allow them to exist.*

Follow your breath, allow it to quiet any and all reactions you might be having from these negative emotions and issues in your being.

As your breath quiets you, notice how the images have disappeared. You are once again surrounded by utter darkness. As you stand in this utter darkness allow one of those early images to appear.*

Allow it to come closer and closer until it floats in front of you. Now look at this negativity, this issue, or feeling which causes you pain. See into the very core of it. Listen to the voice which emanates from it. This voice wants to explain why it is in existence. It wants you to listen, and understand it.

So, do that, listen to the words. Find the understanding.**

After this process is finished, reach out and touch this image. Embrace it. Accept it, for you now understand how and why it was created. You have received clarity, and know there is nothing to fear.

Suddenly, as you stand embracing this image to you, it begins to glow and is filled with a loving light. You find you are dancing and laughing.*

As the movement stills, and all is quiet, share a sacred kiss, and allow this new transformed image to stand beside you.

Face the darkness again. Allow another image to appear.* Watch as it draws closer and closer, until it stands directly in front of you. Now listen to its story and allow the understanding to birth.**

Reach out and embrace this image to you. Accept it, for you now understand this negativity. In your understanding and acceptance of it the transformation begins to take place. It, too, begins to glow and fill with light. Allow the dance and laughter to take place. Rejoice in this new realization. As the movement stills, share the sacred kiss, and have the new, transformed image join you and the first one by your side.

Face the darkness a third time. A third image appears.* It moves closer and closer. If it seems more hostile than the other two, simply allow it to be. It stops in front of you. It stands there waiting, waiting, waiting for you to speak first. Know that it, too, has a story, an explanation for being, but it needs you to ask the first question. So, look at it. Absorb it. Then ask it to please explain itself to you. And listen now to the story as it pours forth. Feel the weeping in its voice.**

As the image finishes its story you find you truly understand it. Without thinking you reach out and embrace it. You find that you are also weeping. The two of you begin to swirl, and in your understanding the image begins to transform, filling with a beautiful rose light. Laughter explodes.

Allow this dance to take place.*

When all is quiet, share the sacred kiss, and have this new, transformed image join you and the other two by your side.

As you stand there within this new freedom of self-expression the darkness surrounds you fast, and without realizing it, a dark hooded shape stands directly in front of you. You can barely make out the shape, and every once in a while a flash of light escapes through the opening of the cape.

You slowly step closer. You are within inches of this hooded figure. Suddenly, from underneath the hood, a brilliant eye peeks out at you, then disappears as quickly as it appeared. You are startled and jump back within the safety of your new self-realized expression.

But as you have jumped back, the cloaked figure has moved forward. You find that you are trembling. Your curiosity is greater than your fear. Hesitantly, but boldly, you reach out, and gently push back the hood of the black cape.

Blinding light illuminates the darkness, and you cannot see for a moment. Blinking, and squinting under the hand you hold over your eyes, shading them from the light, you see a beautiful women standing there. At her feet lies the crumbled, black cape.

She stands in front of you, an image of femininity. She is smiling and beckoning you to come forward. You stand there as if in shock. Your eyes filling with her image.**

You find yourself moving forward into her embrace. As her arms circle round your body you are engulfed in the brilliant light. She begins to twirl and spin with you. And then you hear, inside of you, her beautiful, lyrical voice. She wants to tell you all about herself/yourself; the two of you.

Listen, listen, listen.***

You are drunk with this new awareness. You realize that you are no longer held in her arms, but are lying on the ground. There are no other images around you, only a brilliant light.

You stand and slowly turn round and round, taking in the full space of what use to be darkness. As you turn round and round you begin to perceive that your darkness is really filled with light, and that it is your perception of any given situation which can diminish the light, and cover it up with darkness.

You come to understand that it is okay to have negative emotions, but it is important to take them down into the center of your light, to listen to their story, to understand it, to embrace it, accept it, and then to transform it into light.

You realize that the side of you, which you always thought was evil, is really a beautiful woman hiding inside a black cape, and that she has simply been denied her existence by rejecting the true nature of your being.

You feel your own transformation within the acceptance of your self-expression, your needs, your desires as important. You laugh at yourself now. You laugh because you know there is nothing to fear, and that all darkness can be understood, but first, you must bring the light into it, the light which shines forth with clarity. You are free once more.

Again your Shadow Queen stands before you. You run to her arms, this time embracing her. You laugh into her ears and smile with her gazing into her brilliant blue eyes.

Thank her. Tell her what she means to you.**

The two of you stand entwined in each other's arms. It is time to say farewell, for now. You share the sacred kiss, knowing that it is you who is new and transformed.*

Closing your eyes, feel your body softly floating up. On the breath you rise up, up, up. You carry with you the totality of your experience. You continue to rise, up, up, up - until you touch your center again; the place from where you began this journey.

You rest here for just a moment, tuning into your heart beat, adjusting your ears to the noise around your physical body. With the breath you feel your lungs expand, contract. You feel the hardness of the floor beneath you. You are aware of your physical body and begin wiggling your toes and fingers.

As you lie here, fully aware of your body, in the here and now, your experience is remembered in detail. Breathe naturally and gently for a few more minutes.**

When you are ready, gently open your eyes and allow your body to move.

Know that your Shadow Queen, is indeed, the most beautiful woman of light, and she now lives proudly inside of you.

CHAPTER II

THE MENSUS

The time for re-uniting with our sacredness has come. Let us re-heal our spirits. Let us re-join the true sisterhood. Let us shine forth with our inner power.

We bleed. The ancient mystery blood. The life blood. Not the curse. That is man's name for it. Why? Because they cannot bleed. They realize that unless they bleed they cannot create. They desire to create life just as we do. Because they cannot create they rejoice in taking life, and have come to curse the blood.

When men bleed it is because of one thing, and one thing only: they are injured and will possible die because of the spilling of their blood. Yet, our blood flows freely. Monthly it flows, and we do not die, nor are we injured. So, leave the curse to the men. Re-claim your sacredness - your life blood, and begin looking at it in this new way, in this old light.

We have come to see how women are tied to the moon's cycle. By becoming aware of the moon's cycle you are waking up to the reality that our bodies imitate this cycle. As the crescent appears in the sky our bodies begin to fill with water. Our womb begins filling with the life blood in preparation for conception. As the moon glorifies in its fullness our bodies are ready to receive the seed. We become intensely sensual. We ovulate and release our own life seed, which begins its journey to merge with the male's seed. We are extremely fertile at this time.

If we have not had intimacy with a male at ovulation time, our seed passes from our body. The moon, leaving its fullness and beginning the waning, is the time when our womb begins to cry, releasing the life blood, which is no longer needed. As the moon disappears into darkness our life blood has flowed from us, our bodies have become slender.

At the time of darkness our emotions are acute and we become very sensitive. All the subtle bodies are realigning and the physical body is re-healing, preparing for this process to begin again.

Why do we cramp, get lower back pains, and especially, why do we become irritable? First of all stop and think about it. Isn't your body going through major transitions? So, if your body goes through major transitions, and *will* every single month, why not understand the process and work with it, instead of against it?

The cramping is caused from the blood lining of the womb pulling away to pass, and also the passing of any blood clots, which the lining sometimes forms. The lower pack pain is directly related to the meridian which is located there in direct relationship to the womb. With so much activity going on in the womb the meridian is active and often clouded. The clouding does not allow the natural energy to flow through creating an energy blockage. Irritability is because our hormones are changing.

So, let's work with it.

The first question is if you are on a birth control pill? If you are, it takes quite a bit of juggling to get your mensus on cycle. It can be done. It means being very careful though, because some months you will not take the pill on the last day, and will begin taking your next monthly supply a day earlier. If you decide to have sex on that last day you should use another method of protection, just in case.

However, I do not advise messing around with your birth control pills on your own. If you are not interested in getting pregnant, don't tamper with them.

So, you want to get on cycle. You know that with all your heart. How do you do this? It won't come by staring at the moon, but your awareness of the moon's cycle will help.

Knowledge of herbs will help. There are many books available today which deal with herbs in a holistic manner. Herbs are accessible from health food stores and wholesalers, plus growing your own is a wonderful remedy to having a fresh supply.

Most importantly, attitude helps. This part of your life must become a sacred aspect. Once you come to see it as sacred, and self-empowering, you place it into the category of ceremony – in your mind.

The following tables give a few suggestions to aid you in naturalizing your mensus.

New Moon-Waxing Cycle-Full Moon

Days 2-11
(We need to start with the first visible day of the new crescent which, depending on the month, will either be day two, or day four after dark moon.)

Since this is the waxing phase we do not want to bleed. Now is the time to condition your body into a decrease mensus flow. If your cycle is off balance and you are flowing during this time it is important to follow these steps to encourage your body in returning to its natural cycle.

To Decrease Mensus Flow: Drink one cup (each morning) of one of the following herb teas:
   Comfrey
   Red Raspberry
   White Oak Bark
Or, take one capsule (each morning) of one of the following herbs:
   Golden Seal
   Uva Ursi
1. If you have an altar place a sprig of Mistletoe on it.
2. Burn Bayberry incense daily, or wear the oil.

3. Eat Cayenne pepper with meals.

Other herbs good for this time are: Bistort, Marshmallow, Plantain and Wood Betony. Please note that consuming Bayberry could cause head-aches, and mistletoe is poisonous and could cause nausea and miscarriage if pregnant.

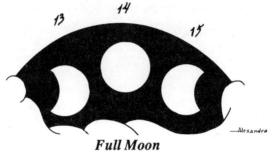

Full Moon

Day 13, 14, and 15

It is important at this time to allow the full moon's influence to come in. Sleep in a place where the moon's light can wash over your face for this three day period. Should this be impossible, sleep with a dim light on, or a candle burning to imitate the Moon's light. Believe me, if you have never been hit in the face by the full moon's light while asleep a candle flame, or soft muted light from a lamp is less light than waking to think the sun is shining in a black sky, or a flood light is coming in your bedroom window.

1. Discontinue drinking the tea, or taking the herb capsules which decrease your mensus.
2. Remove the sprig of Mistletoe from your altar.
3. Discontinue burning Bayberry incense, or wearing the oil.
4. Stop eating Cayenne pepper with your meals.
5. Nightly take a bath allowing your hips and legs to remain continually below the water surface. Sip a cup of red wine or red juice (such as cranberry juice).

This is the interlude. The place where you break the conditioning between waxing and waning. If you are becoming balanced with your cycle you will be fertile during this time and ovulate. Your body will be full and swollen reflecting the Moon. Do not think of your body as being gross, or fat, but rejoice in the womanliness of the curves. Your breasts are full and heavy, your tummy bulges just enough to say "I am woman". Even if your waist and face become a little swollen, allow your Moon Maiden to shine forth. You will be surprised at how appealing you become to your lover at this time, regardless of the water weight.

It wouldn't hurt to start taking some B vitamins. Especially B6, and also C, E, Calcium and Iodine in preparation for the chemical changes your body is about to undergo.

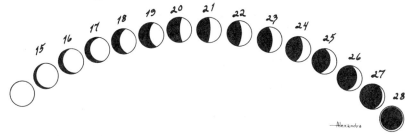

Full Moon-Waning Moon-Dark Moon

Days 16-26

Now is the time it happens. Everything you've been preparing for pays off now with a very sacred closeness to your body and woman power. The releasing of your blood.

To Increase Mensus Flow: Drink one cup (each morning) of one of the following herb teas:

> Chamomile
> Sage

Or, take one capsule (each morning) of one of the following herbs:

> Black Cohosh
> Blue Cohosh

1. Place a sprig of catnip, or Ginger Root on your altar.
2. Burn Sage, or Valerian incense.
3. Eat lots of Parsley, Fennel and Squash with your meals.

Other herbs good for this time are: Brigham Tea (also known as Cramp Bark and Squaw Vine), False Unicorn, Ginseng, Horsetail, Pennyroyal, Safflower, and St. Johnswort. Please note that Blue and Black Cohosh can cause headaches as they are a natural source of estrogen and will depend upon the estrogen level within your own body. If headaches persist discontinue taking these herbs and substitute with Ginseng.

Don Quai is a Chinese herb for the female energy. This herb is great to take at anytime, however, it can put you in contact with your female so much that you want to stay at home and be creative. (Creation is dual for us: Babies, or using our hands: art, baking, sewing, etc. Get the picture?)

The above should be discontinued at the first drop of blood. You now should celebrate your life blood. There are many ways to do this.

Wearing red for the duration of your bleeding is a way of claiming your power while boldly sayings to the world "Red is sacred! Red is powerful! Red is the color of my life blood!"

On the first day of your bleeding, or the heaviest day save a good two-hour block of that day for just you. Celebrate by taking a bath.

Plan ahead for this bath by purchasing red wine or juice to drink, red candles, a red rose, bath salts or oils that feel especially feminine, special music, and a floral incense.

Put your phone off the hook, a "do not disturb" sign on the door, and prepare your water allowing luxurious bubbles and scent to rise from the warmth of the water.

Pour your red wine or juice in a special chalice, put your music on, light your incense and candle. Put your flower in a vase. Grab a great book, and submerge yourself into your special bath honoring you and your sacredness.

...I lay soaking in a warm tub filled with very expensive bubble bath (Chloe, my favorite!). I'm worth the cost of this, I thought to myself. After all, I had bought it just for my celebration bath. I loved the fragrance swirling around my head. It made me feel like a queen.

A silver goblet filled with Rose wine found its way to my lips. The coolness of the wine fell down my throat. "Rhapsody on a Theme of Paganini", the beautiful theme from the movie Somewhere in Time danced in the air. I am a woman. A sensitive, emotional, wonderfully, feminine woman. Tears ran down my face.

I was bleeding, and for the first time in my life I called in sick so that I could honor my blood, and celebrate Me. That was so important to me. To celebrate Me.

So, here I was, early afternoon on a Tuesday. Soaking in a bubble bath drinking wine. My eyes rested on the velvet petals of six red roses.

I let my mind drift. I relaxed in the water. I opened. I lay there until the wine was gone, the water was cool, and side B of the record was ending its third time around.

I smiled at my laziness, slowly got up, and toweled off the excess water dripping from my body. I brushed my hair, put lotion on, anointed several pulse points with jasmine oil, and purposely did not stuff a tampon inside me, or wedge a sanitary napkin between my legs.

I drew a red, silk Japanese kimono on and headed for my sacred temple.

In the middle of the east wall is a window that looks up into the sky. Under the window stood my altar adorned with red cloth. I carried the vase of flowers from the bathroom and placed them in the center of the altar. To either side of the vase sat a red and white candle.

To the front of the altar lay a heavy brown wood framed mirror, resting glass down on the white cloth. I wanted to perform a ceremony for my womanhood. I had worked diligently for three months bringing my body cycle in tune with the moon's. This month I was flowing with that energy.

It was a special day and I wanted to acknowledge that. I was so intensely emotional as I stood there looking down at the altar, that I wept.

There was so much to life, and for so long I had been out of touch. Out of touch with one of the most important aspects of me. Me as woman.

I stood there crying for all the women who were still so far from this special connection. I wept for all the women who had lived and died, and never honored their blood. Suddenly, I knew that I could give women this connection. A smile broke out on my face.

I wiped my eyes and kneeled down in front of the altar. I bowed my head to ground and center. Soon my breath flowed evenly.

I reached to the left of the roses and picked up the white candle. I lit it with a match, then held it up in front of me cradling it in both hands.

"To the Moon," I began.

"It is the energy of this circling orb which pulls on my body, which influences my body. I re-connect my energy to the moon's energy. I open and allow the essence of the moon's cycle to re-align with my own. Together may we wax and wan. Celebrating our fullness. Honoring our emptiness. We are one."

I sat the white flowing candle in front of the roses. The flame stopped flickering and stretched up towards the ceiling, growing long and transparent. In its stillness I found our connection merging.

I placed my hands over my womb feeling the swollen belly protruding.

"To my womb. The place of beginning. The place of transformation. It is here that all my creation births. It is here that my woman energy rests. Within this divinity, within this mystery lives the power of the universe.

"I am a sister with my womb. We share peace from this day forward."

Again tears slid down my face. This time they were tears of reconciliation. Two friends had become re-united. The bond was forming. I joined with the essence of my femininity. I sensed that from this day forward I would be a new woman, and no one, no one would every be able to take that from me.

I reached to the right of the altar, and picked up the red candle. I lowered the wick to the flame of the white one and lit it.

I held it close to my heart peering down in the flame.

"To the blood of my womb. The blood of life. Creative, strong, powerful. Ancient mystery of woman, I celebrate you this day. I am your essence. From me you now flow. I am honored to have this great function of life. No longer are you a curse, or an evil. I rejoice in your pungent smell. I rejoice in your redness. I honor life!"

With the red candle sitting next to the white one I touched my fingers to my vagina. Raising them to my eyes I saw the bright red blood of life staining my fingertips. I wiped the red blood across my face. Re-wetting my fingers a second time I brought them up to my lips and tasted the saltiness.

I stood up and began whirling round in a circle. It seemed as if a part of me had been released. I was no longer held captive by society's negative cage on woman's psyche regarding the blood. I was free.

When my dance slowed, and I melted to the ground before the altar, I picked up the mirror and looked at the wild, painted face staring back at me.

I smiled and said, "Hello Woman!" Then laughed hysterically at how transformed my face looked. It actually beamed with power. With light.

"I am woman," I spoke to the green eyes so alive and twinkling.

"I am sacred woman. Woman who flows with the moon. Woman who bleeds with life blood. Woman who claims her power and feels her energy. Woman who is free and ready to join with other women.

*"I am child, Maiden, Mother, Crone. I am sister, friend, lover. I am the
true essence of Woman, from this day forward, forever more.*

"Blessed Be!"[8]

*The next day I wore red to work. A single red rose stood boldly in a vase
on my desk...*

Ritual is powerful. This is a very sacred time for us. If women would
take control of this time of month, stay within our own dwelling place to
nurture ourselves instead of contending with the workplace, the psyche of
the female would be put to ease.

In olden days women gathered together at this time secluding themselves from the rest of the tribe. It was a time of sacredness. The woman
power was worked with, and the core of the community was secured. It
wasn't until the male population put a stop to this natural and sacred
gathering, that women began to have so many problems with their mensus.

In turn, men started to label it the curse, PMS, and started referring to
women as being a bitch, or on the rag.

Put an end to this negative connotation the male population has placed
upon this most beautiful and sacred monthly function of the female body.
Stop taking the so-called PMS pills man developed, which dis-connects
woman from her power, and drink herbal teas.

If you experience menstrual cramps drink Blessed Thistle, Catnip,
Cramp Bark, Myrrh, Pennyroyal, Peppermint, Red Raspberry or Straw-
berry teas.

If you get lower back pain, then you must lay down; focus your energy
on this part of your body. It is under going quite a lot at this time. Take a
warm bath. Use a heating pad. But please don't perpetuate the male attitude
by rushing to a drug store to buy some PMS pills.

It is your responsibility to claim this sacredness, and stop referring to
it, or seeing it through the male definition.

You are a woman who bleeds for life. Be proud of that. Treasure the
times when you are bleeding. Do not share that energy with man. Try and
find a sister who bleeds at the same time, spend a few hours, a day, or the
complete bleeding with only her.

Watch the changes that take place in you. Feel the power well up within
your heart.

Become sacred again.

It wasn't until several years had passed, after I first performed my blood ceremony, that I received the message it was time to work with women by offering a community ceremony.

With the help of my two apprentices, we began performing the following ceremony for different groups of women in Southern California.

WOMEN WHO BLEED FOR LIFE[9]

Open ceremony by having each woman smudge herself with sage. Then sage the perimeter of the room creating sacred space.

Ground and center the group:

"Close your eyes and with each breath relax your body. Imagine roots extending from your base chakra. Imagine these roots reaching down into Mother Earth. Allow these roots to delve deep into her body until at last they pierce the very core of her. Reach in and draw that pure energy from the Mother up through your roots. Allow it to enter your body through your base chakra. Now embrace that energy in your center. Breathe with this energy for a moment.

"With imaginary branches extending up from your crown chakra, reach up into the heavens. Allow these branches to soar high into Father sky and merge with the universal light. Bring that pure universal energy down through your branches into your crown chakra. Now embrace that energy in your center. Breathe with this energy for a moment.

"Now allow both the nurturing Mother energy of earth, and the universal light energy of Father sky to dance together in your center. Allow these two energies to merge and become one pulsating ball. Breathe this into being.

"Now let your own energy, your essence, merge becoming one with this ball of energy in your center. Know that this pure energy is for your highest good.

"Let this energy grow out, so that it surrounds your body in front and behind you, above and below you.

"Let the energy grow out even more to include all your sisters here in this room, and feel the strength.

"When you are ready, take a deep breath, relax your body, and slowly open your eyes."

Have the women hold hands forming a circle around the altar. (My altar is always placed on the ground. This connection with Mother Earth is vitally important for the type of work I do. The altar I set up for this ceremony is visually beautiful, yet simple. First, I have my Indian blanket folded into a 2' X 2' square, which adds about 4" of height to the center area. On top of this I place a natural fiber mat which is blood red. A red candle is placed on the left side and a white candle is placed on the right side. In the center is an item which represents the female energy. For this ceremony we use a white clay statue of the Moon Goddess with her hands held up over her head. We use the image to hold up to the quarters while invocation.)

Beginning at the east and then moving clockwise invoke the quarters at this point.

> *East:* "To the East I go
> to beckon the power of maidenhood
> the time of life
> before the life blood flows.
> Youth of Maidenhood
> fill us now with purity and the essence of simplicity.
> Be here now.
> So mote it be."

> *South:* "I travel to the South
> The power of first passage of rites.
> The time of bleeding
> when the first drop releases from the womb.
> Innocence of Womanhood,
> flow with us now
> reuniting us with our own remembrance
> to that joyous time.
> Be here now.
> So mote it be."

> *West:* "I come to the West
> to listen to the beating of the heart
> snuggled deep in the womb.

The time of Mothering
when the sacred blood does
form into new life.
Creation of Motherhood grow in us
developing in us with power and sacredness.
Be here now.
So mote it be."

North: "In the North is where I end
fully realized as Woman.
The stillness of wisdom
deep in the soul.
Power of Wise Woman
when the blood no longer flows
united as one with life's mystery.
Be here now.
So mote it be."

East: "To the East I return
completing the circle.
Bowing low to the blood of birth
where our children grow."

The energy has been invoked and all the women present will begin to feel their own internal shifting take place. Now is the best time for giving a lesson. The lesson should be centered/focused on women's connection to the moon cycle, and then the moon cycle and our menstruation connection.

I use Chapter I – The Moon, sections: The Lunar Cycle, The New/ Crescent Moon, Full Moon (omitting the ceremony), and The Dark Moon (omitting the exercise).

I use Chapter II – The Mensus, the three subsections: New Moon-Waxing Cycle-Full Moon, Full Moon, and Full Moon-Waning Moon-Dark Moon, making them into handouts.

After the lesson have the women focus on their womb. Have them lay on their backs with their heads circling the altar. If they bend their knees up, there will not be any pressure on the lower back. Have them place their left hand over the womb center holding it there with the right hand.

A visualization is best here. I use my own experience with the first blood ceremony as retold earlier in Chapter II. I instruct the women to relax, and that when they hear me say "I", to visualize themselves going through the experience. It is a very powerful journey.

After the visualization is complete have the women reach out their hands to the women on either side, placing their hand over the womb. This is a very trusting act. For now each woman has two other females placing their hands on her womb, while she has her hands over their wombs. This is very special for it creates an immediate bonding.

Tell them to relax, and breathe into each others womb. Use a Tibetan bowl, or a singing tube to vibrate above their heads.

Allow the women to open their eyes, and sit up at their own pace. Now is a good time to take a short break.

Now we come to part two of the ceremony. The women are relaxed, in touch with their own womb, and have just bonded with the sisters around them.

This part is for the construction of a Moon Bag. The Moon Bag is a very sacred medicine tool for a woman. It is to be touched by only she who makes it, and should never be placed into the hands of a male.

The Moon Bag itself is made out of red, natural fiber material. Cut a circle about 12 inches in diameter, and with an awl poke twelve holes around the edge, about an inch in. A red cord should be woven through the holes, becoming the draw string to open and close the bag.

The outside of the bag should be adorned in the privacy of ones own home with symbols or beads. We don't have the women adorn the outside in ceremony as it takes a great deal of time. We would rather focus our energy on the inside pouch, and the balance of the ceremony. Because of the time factor we have the red pouches pre-cut and have the women punch the holes in the bag and thread the drawstring through them during this part.

The inner pouch is a small circle of 6 inches. It should be white cotton. On this cloth the women should draw, or write in red paint, or markers symbols which represent their life blood, personal aspects of themselves, which they would not share with anyone else. This cloth should, at some time in privacy, be anointed with their own blood during their next bleeding.

The inner pouch should be filled with herbs, stones, fetishes, and pubic hair. We instruct the women beforehand to bring a stone or fetish which they associate with their bleeding. We allow them the privacy of cutting pubic hair during the ceremony, or they can do it at home.

We provide the following herbs:

     Sage - represents sacredness
     Fennel - toning of the womb
     Ginger Root - spirit of the blood
     Parsley - strengthening of the womb blood
     Chamomile - making peace with the blood
     Red Raspberry - to control the cycle of the blood
     Mistletoe - claiming the right over the blood
     Cayenne - control the spirit of birth

We suggest women choose three to five of the herbs to place in the center of the white circle. They should add their stones, fetishes, and pubic hair, then gather up the white cloth, binding the top with a white cord. This pouch gets placed inside the red bag.

While the women are constructing their Moon Bags it is very important to be focused, and not allow any discussions. To prevent discussions from happening we play percussion instruments, and chant to help the focus, while keeping the energy level up.

Female Energy[10]

"I am female, One with the energy of MaMa earth.
I am female, One with the pull of Moon on tides.
I am female, My body contains the mystery of life and
birth.

"I am female, One with the energy of MaMa earth.
I am female, See how my body waxes and wanes.
I am female, belonging to a Sisterhood of love and
truth.

"I am female, One with the energy of MaMa earth.
I am female, My arms will hold you to heal any hurt.
I am female, The Goddess who protects, our Mother
Earth.

"I am female, One with the energy of MaMa earth.
I am female, One with the energy of MaMa earth.
I am female, Maiden, Mother, Crone, three in one."

We sing this chant over and over until each woman has completed her bag. This is a wonderful energy exchange.

When each woman is finished, we end the chant, then ask all the women to place their bag on the Indian blanket forming a circle around the red place mat. In a kneeling position we place our hands on the ground. (Touch your own thumbs together spread open your fingers, and touch pinky to pinky forming a circle of hands.)

We chant "*Ma-Ma*" allowing the energy to build, directing it into the Moon Bags. Once the cone of power has been released each woman is given a moment to sit back and relax, allowing the energy to integrate. This would be the time for the second and last break.

Now begins the Blood Ceremony. The two altar candles are lit. All other lighting is turned off. The group is brought back together to re-center themselves, feeling the bond between the group and the energy already raised to this point. The time has come for giving thanks to the Great Spirit, Mother Earth, and Father Sky. This can be done quietly.

Now invoke the Goddess, the female energy.

"Mother of life,
power of soul,
womb's life blood
the mysteries flow.

"Mother ancient,
Past, present, future;
we have always known
you are the essence
of a woman's glow.

"Come now,
to our open hearts
Come now,
to our blood flow.

Of vein or womb
it does not matter which
Come now Mother,
and unite us once more."

The energy will definitely switch, and for those of you with the sight you will now see the room fill with the presence of the Grandmothers.

We share a beautiful song at this time, singing it together gathered round the altar.

Woman Power[11]

"It is to the Sisterhood we return at last
Always propelled by Woman Power.
It is the Goddess we at last ask in our hearts
Always compelled by Woman Power.

"To the depths of our soul we wander as if lost
Seeking a grander side of our life.
Standing at the threshold we see within our light
A beautiful Woman shining with power and might.

"It is to the Earth we turn to connect with
Always encouraged by Woman Power.
It is to humanity we seek to hold and love
Always sustained by Woman Power."

As the song comes to a close each woman will be transformed, an angelic smile on her lips. Her face will glow, and gentleness will rise.

Gently have the women move to one side of the room. Here, Lisa begins playing the singing sticks in a constant clack-clack-clack. I remain at the altar. With back turned to the women I give thanks to the Grandmothers for being present, then turn and motion for one of the women to come up to the altar, and sit facing me.

I hold up a red votive candle in a scallop shell, and inform her that by accepting the candle, and lighting it on the red altar candle, she will be making an act of power. The act of power of taking responsibility for her agreement to come into this life in the female body. I instruct her to light the candle, and say silently or verbally, an affirmation sitting on the altar. After she lights the candle, says her affirmation, she is to set the candle down on the ground around the Indian rug, and return to her seat with the other women.

This is a very private moment. Some women speak quietly in their own hearts. Some boldly speak out. As the last woman lights her candle and places it in the last spot available on the ground, a glowing circle is completed around the Indian rug, a ring of Moon Bags circling the inner red place mat, and the center of the altar with the two altar candles and the Moon Goddess image. It is a breathtaking sight.

I gather all the women around the altar and while Lisa continues to play the singing sticks we say the affirmation out loud over and over again until it rings in the air.

Affirmation[12]

"I am Woman, I am, I flow
I am Whole, I am, I know
I am Power, I am, I grow"

Smiles break out and we have a group hug. The women are ready to take control of their body, connecting fully with their female essence.

Once again have the women return to the far side of the room to group together. Gail begins shaking a rattle. I turn my back a second time to the women and sing my Power Chant to the Grandmothers. When I am ready I beckon the first woman forward. Instantly Gail and Lisa begin a chant which will last the entire time.

Acceptance Chant[13]

"I accept my power willingly
We become one, we become one.
I use it for the highest good
We become one, we become one.
Now I walk my path of power
We become one, we become one.

Through the Mother I am my power
We become one, we become one."

As each woman sits before me I hold up a mortar which contains the blood of the Mother (I use red ocher).

"This is the blood of the Mother, ever are we mindful there can be no birth without the spilling of the life blood.
"Since we are women who bleed, let us merge our life blood with each other, and restore the power and mystery of Womanhood."

I ask each woman, "Do you accept your power?" After she answers "yes", with the tips of the first and second fingers of my right hand I dip them in the blood and look each woman in the eyes. I speak her name, and allow the Grandmothers to bestow a promise, then mark her face with the blood.

I mark the left wrist and have her press both wrists together. As each woman returns to her seat she will repeat the wrist merging with the woman before and after her. Soon a string of women sit, side by side, with their wrists held together.

After each woman is anointed I mark my own face. I pick up my drum and join Gail. Lisa joins in with the singing sticks. We begin chanting, "We are now one."

At this point it is important for the women to dance their power. With the percussions and chanting still going on have the women begin to move. Turn on music which is very rhythmic and has the feeling of tribal dancing in the jungle. Allow the instruments to diminish and the jungle music to take over. Allow the women to dance for a good ten minutes.

We move in a moon-wise circle as this is the direction the female energy flows in. I yell out directions every so often such as "feel your female", "dance your bond to sisterhood", "become one with Mother Earth", and so on.

The dance is ended by stopping in place and turning to face the center. Movement should be slow and swaying. When movement comes to a complete stop instruct the women to slap their hands together, rub their palms back and forth quickly, blow their breath of spirit on the palms, and draw that energy into their power center by covering their womb area with their palms.

We fill with the energy, and then bend down, placing our palms on the ground, giving back to the Mother the balance of the energy.

A moment of silence is now needed. As each woman comes to a sitting position, we end the ceremony with a chant.

Life Blood Chant[14]

"I am the mystery that flows
My beginning is from Life's pool
I am the mystery that creates
My veil unfolds with New Moon
I am the mystery that counsels
My remembrance in faces new
I am She who bleeds, I am she who bleeds."

The Goddess is then thanked. Mother Earth and Father Sky are thanked. The Great Spirit is thanked. Then each woman gives thanks to herself for being here, and loving herself enough to allow this aspect of her being to become re-connected. The quarters are then dismissed. Beginning in the east and moving clockwise.

East:"Birth, Maidenhood, first life blood
You are in us, we are in you.
Blessed be."

South:"Womanhood, releasing the flow
We are sisters forever more.
Blessed be."

West:"Mother full of life
Cradled by soft warm blood
This was our beginning
Woman and man alike.
Blessed be."

North: "Wise Woman at the end of life
Tough the blood has ceased
The power of mystery grows.
Blessed Be."

We open the circle with the traditional sayings:

"The circle is open, but ever unbroken.
May the love of the Goddess go in our hearts.
Merry meet, and merry part,
And merry meet again.

"This rite has ended."

Of course no circle would be complete without hugs and kisses.

I give you permission to duplicate this ceremony and use it as many times as possible. Should you be a creative woman, and enjoy writing your own ceremony, then you have got a wonderful guideline to use.

If you write a new ceremony, please send me a copy and I will give more life to it.

After performing a solo or group ceremony, you have danced your first passage of rites, and are an honored woman. What a wonderful act of power!

PART TWO

The Sisterhood

THE SISTERHOOD

Let us weave the circle
as in ancient times
standing side by side
holding hands
becoming one.[1]

...It was a beautiful, early summer day. Fifteen women were traveling from various cities to attend a Womanhood Celebration which was to take place in a cathedral of oak tree's, out in the solitude of Casper's Park.

A dear friend had decided to go and rode with me to the park an hour before the specified gathering time. I needed to mark the trail to the oak grove and set up circle.

The sun was beautiful that morning as we set out. A cloudless sky canopied above. Excitedly we talked about the ceremony. She had never before attended a woman's circle and was nervous. I explained to her the meaning behind the ceremony; that seemed to calm her.

In silence we took in the different shades of green as we drove east on Ortega Highway.

We rolled down our windows allowing the fresh air inside the car. Already the air held a tension of transformation. My nerves tingled as they came in contact with the energy in the air. Most of the women coming together were unknown to each other. I didn't know what to expect and surrendered any apprehension I might feel over to the power of Womanhood.

Obviously, we were all meant to share this experience no matter what level of awareness we stood upon, or what our belief systems might be.

At last we pulled into the entrance of the Park. I got out of the car to pay the attendant for the seven cars which would be arriving and were part of our party.

The young, blond attendant was somewhat frazzled as he had been out drinking the night before and was wearing a hangover headache, but found the humor to smile as I teased him. He rewarded me with a beautiful owl feather. An omen for the day. (Yes, I would rely on my second sight to get me through this day.)

We drove to the furthest point we could, parked the car, and unloaded the materials to be carried to the grove, a ten minute hike from where we parked. Not a soul in sight. We locked the car and headed up the trail tying purple ribbons every ten feet or so.

We marveled at how dry the area already was; so early in the season. The scent of sage and wormwood tickled our noses. Jack rabbits darted out from under brush, scampering to get out of our way. Hawks flew over head and bee's were everywhere amongst the clover. It was already hot and only ten o'clock in the morning. I was glad we would be under a canopy of tree foliage for the ceremony.

At last we arrived at the entrance to the ancient elfin grove of oaks. The stillness of the air stopped me when we walked into the large domed camp. It was so quiet. Usually when I walked into the grove I got such an other-worldly feeling, and would catch flashes of movement everywhere.

But the magical camp fires and sparkling lights did not instantly disappear the moment we walked within the camp; the elfin occupants scurrying to hide their presence. In fact, this time, there was no sign of them. A hush in the middle of the celebration did not suddenly jolt the senses into the feeling of having intruded on some ancient tribe of people.

No, instead it was quiet and still. Devoid of any magic at all. Well, we'll fix that, I thought.

"I feel we should set the circle up over here," I said to Mary as I continued into the center of the camp.

"It seems pretty level, and last time I was here I found a beautiful crow feather resting in the center spot."

Mary bent over and picked up another crow feather in almost the exact spot I had found the other one. We laughed at the irony of it. Needless to say, she agreed on the spot with me.

As I sat up the altar Mary went off to collect feathers. I watched her for a moment among the brush, her step crunching dry oak leaves. A lost child of this time, but so at rest in the woods. I turned my attention back to the business needing attention.

Unpacking the items we had carried from the car, I made a mound of corn meal and placed the South Crystal on it. Then drew a circle of corn meal twelve inches out from the crystal to indicate the altar area. Around the center crystal I laid small seed crystals, which would eventually be given to each of the women attending.

Mary returned with a dozen black bird feathers and arranged them around the seed crystals. The final touch was a circle of roses, pansies and wild flowers scattered around the completed altar.

We stood back and looked at the altar taking in the beauty of it; the power from the natural elements. We smiled at each other and finished marking the circle by placing small bunches of flowers nine feet out from the center in each of the quarters.

Mary found a nice spot to arrange blankets to sit on after the ceremony, and I found a tree to hang a sheet over a branch and a roll of toilet paper should anyone need to relive themselves.

Our work done we headed back up to the grandfather oak which was to be the gathering area. Gail and Lisa were there with the rest of the women.

We had a moment of breathing and silence to feel the park, to let down any barriers that might exist because of nerves and expectations. Each woman took in her surroundings while casually eyeing the other women gathered.

When it felt right I stepped forward.

"Thank you for being here with us today. We would like to introduce ourselves. Women Spirit Rising of Costa Mesa is an organization of women, and this is the first of many sponsored events for us.

"Our dream is to take WSR, obviously as far as it can go, but primarily to provide a spiritual learning center for women, and maybe eventually men, that will include more activities such as this one. Also to provide a

networking referral system, workshops, festivals, guest speakers, full and new moon circles, classes on esoteric studies, and on-going bi-monthly spiritual gatherings which would include toning, movement, visualization, sharing of traditions, etc., etc.

"So you see, we have a lot planned for WSR. It can only grow, and your involvement, and bringing other women into our ever-widening circle will contribute to that dream and help it grow."

I looked around at the faces staring at me. I wasn't sure if I had reached them as some women looked bored. Maybe, I'm talking too much, I thought to myself as I glanced at Gail and Lisa for reassurance. They were smiling.

Gail stepped forward and was speaking about her beliefs and hopes for WSR, and then Lisa took up where Gail left off. This gave me a moment to study the women gathered, their eyes no longer on me.

Most of the women appeared to be very masculine. Hair cut short, jaws held sharp. Clothing were pants, t-shirts and tennis shoes. Only two other women, beside Lisa and me, wore skirts. That's okay, I told myself. Most of the women I would be put in touch with would be women who had lost touch with their female energy. So, this was okay.

Their eyes turned back to me. I glanced at Gail and Lisa. Oh, yes they had finished their parts and had given me my cue to speak my personal belief. I giggled, made some remark about being put on the spot, then looked at the ground.

"Women Spirit Rising," I began still looking at the ground, "is not only a networking for the esoteric community, but a sisterhood for women." I stopped to let this sink in and see if there were any reactions. Blank faces stared at me. Okay.

"When women come together and bond...allowing their energies to merge, the power that is created becomes the foundation of our lives. That foundation not only heals us physically, but spiritually as well. Together we all become stronger.

"In working with the sisterhood it has not only been a dream come true for me, but a very much needed part of my life. The woman that I am today has only been enhanced by Lisa and Gail, and the strength and support created by them.

"I am very pleased to have sisters like them, and to have a sisterhood. We want to open this to all women." Lisa and Gail hugged me. I smiled at the other women.

"So, are you ready to have ceremony?" Verbal assents flew from every direction.

"Follow me." I waved them up, turned and headed down the path a hundred or so yards, stopping to point out herbs of interest; especially poison oak.

I came to a halt just outside the entrance to the oak grove. A snake of fifteen women lay on the path. I turned and faced them.

"Through women you were born into this world. Through women you will be born into this circle."[2]

With that I took hold of Mary's hands and raised them over our heads creating an archway. Lisa went through first. As the second woman passed through, Lisa took hold of her hands, raised them above their heads continuing the arch.

Soon we had a tunnel of women's arms. Mary and I stood at the end. We broke our hold and passed through the tunnel. This process went on until the tunnel brought us just inside the camp.

For a third time Mary and I stood at the end. We broke hold and walked down through the tunnel. As we formed the arch on the other end I began reciting blessings to each woman as she passed.

"Of woman you are born." "Blessed Mother of all things." "Rejoice in your birth into the sisterhood of life." Soon several women joined in the blessings.

And when it was my turn to walk through the tunnel, the feeling of receiving the blessings while walking through a womb of arms was amazing. There was a sense of security and compassion. I came to the end of the tunnel and kept walking. In turn, as each woman passed through the tunnel for the final time, they followed me until, at last, we all stood around the beautiful altar in the middle of the cathedral.

I pointed out the make-shift toilet, and the blanket area where they should set their belongings. Then we began the ceremony by smudging ourselves with sage. When the abalone shell containing the burning leaves, and the beaded prayer feather was returned to me, I walked to the east and circled around the women clockwise marking the boundary of sacred space.

Lisa grounded and centered us. Gail called in the quarters. Our circle was cast. The women were told to hold hands, close their eyes and tune into their breathe. As the natural rhythm of breath took over they were told to sense the group breath and begin breathing as one.

Lisa, Gail and myself stood in the center of the women around the altar. Together we began giving thanks.

"Before ever land was, before ever the sea,
or soft hair of the grass, or fair limbs of
the tree, or flesh colored fruit of Her
branches, She was, and our soul was in She.

"She is the star that rises from the twilight sea.
She brings women dreams to rule their destiny.
She is the eternal woman. She is She. The tides
of all souls belong to Her. These are the moon tides,
these belong to She."[3]

In the silence I looked up as a stream of sunlight found an opening in the olive green foliage; dancing down on the center of the altar. A light wind shook the branches, oak leaves gently fell around us. I closed my eyes. Took a moment to let the energy settle. Opening my eyes I looked at Gail and Lisa. We continued.

"Our Father who art in Heaven
hallowed be thy name. Thy kingdom come,
Thy love be born on Earth as it is in
Heaven. Give us this day thy holy strength.
Inspire our divine forgiveness, so that we may
forgive the trespasses of all relations on Earth,
and guide us down the Beauty Path, so we may walk in
light once more."[4]

The cawing of a crow was heard overhead, and once again the wind shook loose leaves to fall upon us.

"The One Power that moves the moon, moves through us. The power that lights the sun lights our life. It is female and it is male.

"It is clouds and rain. It lives in the damp earth. In root and in bud. It moves the wind. It is all life, born and unborn, on this plane and in the next.

Visible and invisible. In planet and star.

"It is infinite, it blesses and protects, heals and creates. It moves backwards and forwards in Time, through all of space, in this life, and in myriad others yet to come, and in the past as well.

"This power is yours as it is mine. It is the Goddess and it is God. It is the Child. It is the Universe."[5]

The three of us closed our eyes for a moment and joined the breath of the group. Simultaneously we moved out of the center, in different directions, and broke into the circle of women.

Together the women felt the break and opened their eyes. They were high. I looked across the circle and smiled deeply at Jade Wind Woman. Her spirit was standing straight up. She smiled back. I let my eyes move from woman to woman and connect. Only one woman refused to look at me.

I could see the rigidity of her body and knew she would be the most difficult energy of the day. We always have a challenge, I mused.

Dropping the hands of each woman on both sides, I walked over and picked up the darbuka drum and began drumming. I took the women into the clockwise circle dance. We began to chant:

"Oh come, Holy Mother
Oh come, Holy Father
Oh come, Holy Child
Our hearts and the heart of the Earth are One."[6]

Slowly, we moved round. As the chant ended Lisa took us into the "I Am" chant. The women seemed to resist the learning of the movements so we sang the words over and over.

As the familiarity with the chant developed in each woman, my focus was brought out of the circle. I began singing to the earth and all the living creatures being drawn to our circle.

A baby rattle snake, twenty yards off to the west, announced its presence; continuing to interject from time to time when the stillness of the group permeated the oak grove.

All movement and all chanting came to a stop. Some women were visibly shaken by having to move out in an open area. Their inhibitions were up and they found themselves uncomfortable.

I spoke to them about our child within. How this child needed to be set free. By keeping our child smothered, our body begins to crystallize and we find all our joints becoming stiff. We age very quickly when this happens. I told them the child longs to dance and celebrate, and it was the ego, the mind, which puts fear in place of this natural part of our being. I had the women form a tight circle around the altar, wrapping their arms around each other. Then closing their eyes, once again I urged them to concentrate on their own breath first and then the group breath.

Quietly I walked around them, outside of the circle, waiting for their fear to subside. Waiting for the breath to become quiet and natural.

"We have come beyond the beliefs of childhood to a stage in our lives where it is time to know who we are and how we are in relation to other things and to be aware of our choice. Destiny is a matter of our thinking. Life unfolds in the world around us, and our interaction is a part of its unfolding. So the world situation is not happening to us; situations are the result of our collective thought and action.[7]

"Know that you are not "coincidentally" here. You chose to be here, to be a part of this ceremony today. Your spirit needs to experience this ceremony as a form of awakening a sleeping part of your being.

"We are the days and we are the nights and we are the stars. We are holy beings.[8] We are women."

I felt spirit come into me and take over. I continued to speak to the women about putting an end to the animosity between us. To stop weakening the sisterhood by finding fault with a sister, or turning away only to stab her in the back.

I circled round and round, and threw questions at them. Questions such as "why don't you want to touch the woman to your right at this moment?", or "what benefits do you receive when you complain about another woman and call her a bitch?"

I spoke from the heart, from my female power center. I was strong and over-powering. I could see some women visible cringe when I touched upon the issues they were guilty of.

Round and round I walked spinning a web of energy. A web that pressed in on them. There was no place for them to hide. Then I let it fall on their shoulders.

"It is up to you to stop the quarreling and separation between women. Stop now. Connect with another woman on a regular basis. Form a small group which meets every week, or a couple times a month. Don't put a woman down in front of a man. Support your sister. Stop gossiping about a woman you feel at odds with. Instead make the effort of understanding her motives and why your buttons are being pushed. Then make peace with her."

I stopped behind a woman I had worked with. She and I had been guilty of this type of relationship. Yet, deep down inside we had always stood by each other when it really got rough. I was fond of Shelley, and so very happy she had found the courage to come to the ceremony this day.

"Open your eyes now. Let the lesson which turned into a lecture rest inside of you, but let it go for now."

There was a little nervous laughter from different women. I bent over and picked up a spool of red yarn and held it up as I joined the circle.

"Mother Earth feeds us through the invisible umbilical cord. Qualities of energy arise from her bosom entering our navels as sound energy for each organ system.[9]

"We are born connected to the life force of our own Mother by the umbilical cord.

"This," I waved the scan of yarn over my head. "Is the umbilical cord of the Goddess, of the female, of the Sisterhood."

I began unraveling the yarn. "I am going to have Lisa take this yarn and wrap it around your waist." Lisa came over to me and took the spool from my hands. I held onto the end of the yarn as she moved left wrapping it around each woman.

"Open yourself to the connection with the Mother – all mothers. And allow the merging of spirit with your sisters to take place."

When Lisa returned to my side I wrapped the yarn around her waist and cut the spool away. I held the two ends together. We began a "Ma-Ma" cone of energy allowing the cord and the connection to become complete.

When the chorus of voices left the air and silence lingered around the circle, I opened my eyes and looked at the new family standing before me.

Everyone returned my smile.

"As we are all connected with Goddess, and one as Women, we must remember that we must also stand alone at times becoming a strength and power of the Sisterhood, a unique part of the whole."

With that I began moving around the circle, cutting the cord between each woman so that they had a piece of the cord to take with them.

The energy was soft and nurturing. A shower of leaves fell around us. A jogger swept by, craning over his shoulder as he passed to see what we were doing.

We automatically came into a group hug and laughed at his unspoken sense of being left out. A middle-aged woman wanted to share a simple affirmation with us. Everyone was willing for her to speak.

"It is very simple," Jane said as we stood embracing in a full stream of sunlight which had originally been small, but having found a hole in the foliage filtered down to spotlight our unity.

"I am love, I am love, I am love," she sang. Instantly we picked up the melody and stood singing, swaying our bodies to it. We were connecting on all levels. All barriers were down. No one was afraid anymore. In some inner way each woman had made peace with all the women in the world. There was no need for feeling jealous or competitive toward another woman. We were one, and all women were one. We ended with our heads together. Our focus turned now to the altar of the circle below us.

The altar was waiting to give-away its beautiful gifts. Each woman was asked to bend down and chose one of the seed crystals and blackbird feathers to take as a connection to the energy worked with, and as a reminder that in her everyday life it was her responsibility to keep the ceremony and bond between women alive. It was a special moment. After each of us picked our gift we stood there holding them up to the sunlight and each other.

Gail gave thanks to Goddess, God and Universal Life Force. Then she dismissed the quarters and opened circle.

We adjourned to the blankets were cakes and wine awaited us. Soon the oak grove was filled with chattering as our conversations took over.

For the first time in many of their lives, a sense of the true meaning of the word "sisterhood" became clear; a reality. The Womanhood Celebration had been a success...

CHAPTER III

THE HEALING

We must heal ourselves, and then we must help others heal. As women we must heal the pains of childhood; that wonderful map to our enlightenment.

We help create our own reality, and we are born into this world after having made such an agreement. That agreement consists of:

1) taking the body of female, and the female energy;
2) taking a family structure, whether it be good or bad to learn lessons not learned before.

There are no victims in life. It is when you forget part of your agreement, and delve into the "poor little me" syndrome that you become a victim. A victim of your own circumstance.

I have worked privately with many women who have forgotten their agreement. Most of them fall into three categories: Father neglect, Denial of female, and Fear of God.

In each case the woman has smothered her energy, given it away, or simply never awakened it.

FATHER NEGLECT

Father neglect happens in many ways: sexual misconduct, complete dismissal/lack of affection, or child-beating. In each instance the child is never given a father role model who is healthy, and so either looks outside of the family for one, or begins believing that her father is normal and their relationship is normal.

Fortunately most of the women I have worked with have had a satisfactory, or more than satisfactory relationship with their mothers, but since the mother figure has chosen to live in a situation with a neglectful husband/father role the child learns co-dependency from her mother. And by the time the child grows into a woman she has learned to give all her power away as her mother did, making her relationships with men her act of power. She does this because she so desperately longs to be loved by the men in her life in a way her father never did.

The woman from a family such as this comes to see love as a bargain, or manipulation. Love is associated to negative energy, and sometimes the only way to get the attention she is used to with a male is by being a bad little girl.

Often times memories of childhood are too painful for a woman of the above experience to look at. Some, if not most, know why they cannot have a healthy relationship today. It takes a real act of courage to want to heal this type of childhood pain. For the woman must be willing to revisit that time and become her child once again.

If she doesn't heal this pain of childhood her adult relationships with men will be unhealthy. She will remain the weakling in her relationships. She will give all her power away to the man. He becomes, in essence, her act of power. Often you will hear her claim she will die if he isn't by her side.

Men become very confused in this type of relationship. Men walk the face of this earth looking for their "Goddess." Their woman who will help show them how to live on Mother Earth, how to become balanced with this already foreign energy they felt from day one. When they come into a relationship where the woman is such a weakling and drools every time she looks at the man, or rests all her decisions on him, he feels lost.

The next thing you know the male ego kicks in to hide the insecurity he's feeling, and there you have it; the masculine energy saturates the relationship, and now everyone involved is off balance. The relationship turns sour, and begins to struggle.

I know some people may read my theories and say, "it isn't that simple", but you know, if we stop and take a look at the most basic, the most simple underlining facts then we would heal ourselves and others a lot faster.

The facts in the above situations are:

1. I made an agreement to be a female body/energy in this life.

2. I made an agreement to be raised in an environment where I have a poor, or non-existent father/male role model.

3. I made an agreement to learn, as a child, that if the female is weak in a relationship she will choose a mate who is off-balance and who becomes abusive.

4. I made an agreement to learn, as a child, that as a female it is my responsibility to help by changing this pattern. The way to help is not be a weakling when I grow up.

5. I made an agreement to learn, as a child, that if the female gives her power away there can be no balance in a relationship.

6. I made an agreement, as a child, to learn that a relationship is not an act of power, that becoming your own essence is. By first becoming your own essence then the healthy relationship can follow.

How can a child know all this? Our spirit does. Our conscious knows what is right or wrong. We chose how we are going to handle every given situation. It is all part of the lesson. It is karma.

We either learn right the first time, or we keep going through the same situation under different circumstances until we get it right.

It is a lot easier to learn the garbage as a child. Then we have the rest of this life to enjoy the fruits of our labor, and...begin the next lesson.

The following is an outline I use when working with women of the above situation. It is a basic session many therapists use today. It can be done alone, but it would be best to do it with a person who is familiar with this technique and can guide you through it.

Remember, we have the ability to heal ourselves. If we make the commitment we can do it alone. It simply means you are ready to begin giving up your co-dependency. Only you can make the first step.

Only you know when it is essential to have another person assist you in breaking through a block. It is at those times that you should seek out that person. However, I believe synchronicity is part of the universe's way of opening doors to us. When you are truly ready and it is the right time all things come together smoothly and easily.

I call this the Relationship Meditation. It is important to allow a couple of weeks, or months to go through each part of the outline.

Relationship Meditation

Part I: The Pains of Childhood

1. Completely relax yourself. Center. Allow yourself to focus on relationships; father, mother siblings, mates, friends, etc. Have the willingness to heal, to understand why, to forgive, and allow any and all negative emotions, or scenes from your childhood, and in current relationships to come up. Remember, give yourself permission to experience this.

2. Make a Child Pain list. Write down any and everything the child experienced during the above exercise. This list will include the eventual willingness, and acceptance of the child to equally participate in the unhealthy relationship, which has caused you to now feel guilty. The guilt which makes you blame yourself that it was your fault, or that you enjoyed it. Remember, you were only a child who in a state of innocence was betrayed by an adult.

Part II: The Childhood Journey

1. Relax completely, and center. Allow yourself to be taken back to the crucial age of your childhood when you accepted and became part of the unhealthy relationship.

2. Revisit and speak with those people who influenced you. Invoke those same emotions you were experiencing as a child. Know that if you take awakened consciousness back with you, child will be able to say "no". Child will be able to understand the perversity of the situation.

3. After the child has established healthy and protected relationships with those who had previously influenced her, bring the child back up through the ages retaining this new understanding, this new awareness.

4. As a woman/adult in the now, bring each of those people to mind so you can tell them, face to face, how they once harmed you. Tell them how you wanted to trust them, and be loved by them. Tell them how they

betrayed the innocence of your child. Tell them how sick and off-balance they were. Then tell them they cannot harm you any more. You have broken their spell, and you are free to become whole and balanced.

5. Come back to the here and now. Make a new list. A Woman's Healing list. Write down all the positives you feel, and the lesson learned in relationship with those people. (Remember, you can do the above alone, but if you know someone who can assist you it is advisable, because then you can do role playing which enhances this meditation.)

Part III: Releasing Ceremony

1. When ready to release this aspect of your childhood from your adult life take your Child Pain list and your Woman's Healing list and go somewhere where you can be alone.

2. Find a spot that feels powerful to you. Stand or sit there. Relax yourself. Ground and center. Then begin letting your power in. As this new power fills you let it shine through every pore so that you are beaming with the light of this power.

3. Take your Child Pain list and hold it up in your hands. Speak loudly and boldly and tell the Great Spirit of Life how you have battled the lesson of childhood, and won. Tell the Great Spirit how you have killed the negative energy which held you in its grasp. Allow yourself to chant, or be there for a moment with this new victory. Then when you are ready tear this list up into tiny pieces. Bury it, burn it or drown it in water, and release it back to the universe. Back to the place of agreement.

4. Collect yourself. Take up your Woman's Healing list and hold it up in your hands. Tell the Great Spirit how positive you are now, how you see and feel the learning taking place. Tell the Great Spirit that you have fulfilled an agreement to this life and are happy that you have learned. Chant or dance or just be your learned lesson, your healing. Then when you are ready tear this paper into four parts. Hold each of the parts (individually) up to each of the four quarters giving thanks for your achievement. Then bury, burn or place in the water each part.

5. Now give thanks to all of life. Give thanks to yourself.

Part IV: Forgiving Ceremony

1. As a woman healing her childhood pain, it is important to now forgive those people who harmed you as a child. Unless you can come to forgive

them you will carry the residue of the pain for the rest of your life.

2. Relax and center yourself. Allow your mind to quiet and when you're ready go to a very special place within. Call each person to you. When you feel their presence tell them you are now able to forgive their trespassings. Tell them why you can forgive them. Tell them you understand the illness which had overcome them; that it was part of your agreement. Then let them go.

3. When you have forgiven the others turn to your own heart and call forth the image of your little girl. Take her in your arms and hug her close to your body. Tell her you forgive her, that you understand now. Help her to smile and return the hug.

4. After you have finished with your little girl come back to the here and now. Have by your side a mirror, or get up and go look in one. As you look at your face in the mirror smile at yourself. Look into your own eyes. Say your own name. Then tell your image "I love you."

Remember, do this entire meditation over a period of days, weeks, or months. Do it at your own pace, and only when you are ready to "clean" house.

DENIAL OF FEMALE

Denial of female is just that. A spirit who is born in the body of female and refuses to accept this basic fact of life.

As children they were tom-boys. As women they are aggressive, impostors of men. Most often these women carry extra weight on their bodies, cut their hair short, and search for jobs/careers where they must compete with men and outshine those men for the position they desire.

Women who deny their female, become so competitive with men that they try to become "one of the guys", and will go to any length to prove that they are not a "typical woman", who, in their opinion, cries, is dumb, and weak.

Often this woman will not have time to get together with the girls, and so becomes a recluse, or often hangs out with the guys from the office.

If in relationship she will be domineering, and find a mate who is weaker than she is. Though she desperately seeks a man who is a "real man". (Meaning: a man who would not hesitate to put her in her place.)

First of all, if you are a woman who denies, or partially denies her female body/energy you need to take a moment now to center yourself.

Remember you made an agreement to come into this life and inhabit a female body. You walk on a planet that is female energy, and yet you are doing everything out of your power to change that and be male.

Female is not weak. In fact, female is very strong. Being true to your own essence, your true energy, is an act of power beyond the imagination.

By accepting your female energy and embracing this physical body you dwell within, you will not lose anything from life nor will you be denied the job you desire or the dreams you fantasize.

The true movement of women's liberation was not about becoming a man. It was about being acknowledged as a woman. A woman who has a soul, and a heart, and a rightful place to participate in the worldly arena of life.

One of our Grandmothers who was brave enough, stood up for all women at the first Woman's Right Convention held in Seneca Falls, New York in 1848, Elizabeth Cady Stanton. It is her brilliant, but simple words spoken in her conclusive statement on that day we should hearken to:

"...self-development is a higher duty than self-sacrifice and should be a woman's motto hence-forward." [10]

I'm all for equal benefits but do you honestly think you are proving your worth and equality by denying your female (female energy)?

No. In fact what you are doing when you deny (your female) and become an imposter of the male is actually broadcasting that you think they are superior than you. You are giving out the signals that you surrender to them. That in order for you to be classified "good enough" to work beside them, you must "pretend" not to be a female. Isn't that silly?

When you make the conscious choice to re-claim your power by embracing your essence – your female energy – you awaken your power center within you. The strength and support of Mother Earth's energy is then able to flow back into this center and merge.

Suddenly, you will find, that you can stand on your own merits. The merits of simply being a woman.

There is a very old ritual that was performed and celebrated in women's mysteries. It is a "self-blessing".[11] It is a woman's blessing on herself; honoring her female energy. This ritual is only the beginning step, and one must remember that any doubts or fears must be cleared from the mind before beginning. You will experience a cleaning-out of psychic debris after performing this ritual. Once a cleaning has taken place it is important to focus the mind and psyche on the new energy you wish to flow through you. I would like to give the ritual outline (as explained) from one woman's personal experience.

...Lisa was now ready to embrace her female. She had existed half in and half out of her agreement to inhabit the female body. She wanted to merge and become whole. She asked me to take her through the self-blessing ceremony. She said she was ready.

Upon arriving at my home one evening I asked Lisa to walk around the living room and chose an item which represented the female energy to her. She chose a six inch pot of rose geraniums. I took the plant and handed her a red silk kimono to change into.

"No underclothing, or jewelry." I instructed her. Then left her to go set up the circle.

I entered the special room I use for meditation and ceremony, and began setting up the altar Lisa would be using. I placed the geranium in the center of the altar. To either side of the plant I put two white tapers. In front of the plant I put a platter of salt and a beautiful crystal chalice with a gold plated vine design on the outside of it. I filled the chalice with a mixture of water and wine.

I heard a quiet knock on the door and rose to open it. Lisa stood timidly in the hall. I smiled at her, she nervously returned one, then I hugged her to me.

"Lisa, look around the room." She did.

"I would like you to chose the quarter you want your altar to be placed in." She looked at me then began moving. She stopped in the west. Turning to look at me she said "Here."

I carried the altar over to the west and placed a large pillow down in front of it. Turning to Lisa I motioned for her to stand next to me.

"You chose a green plant to represent your female. You are like the virgin. Brand new in your discovery of self. Wild and free like nature. Ready to grow and bloom like the herb before you."

Lisa was happy with her choice and finally smiled, relaxing.

"You choose the west. The place of water. This is where the power of woman dwells. This is the emotion of the heart, the deep darkness of the intuition. This is the place of death and rebirth. You have chosen well Lisa."

She beamed with satisfaction.

"Now, stand before your altar. I will direct you. Do not interrupt but should you have a question then listen to the answer which your heart gives you. Okay?" I looked at her. She nodded yes.

She took her place before the altar. I went and sat down before the permanent altar of the room in the east. I lit a candle, turned off the lights. Shadows from the one flame filled the room. The alteration of atmosphere immediately took place.

"Breathe. Smoothly, deeply. Follow the natural rhythm of your breath into your heart, into your womb, into your feet. Feel as every inch of you tingles with the life force of your breath.

"Before you is a platter of salt, the symbol of Mother Earth. Pick it up and hold it arms length in front of you." She did as she was told. "Look at this salt, look at the Mother. From her all source of power flows. From Her all wisdom flows. Place a pinch of the earth on the pillow before you and then kneel down upon it."

Lisa performed the task, then kneeled down on the pillow.

"Lisa know that you are kneeling on your own power, and your own wisdom. You may put down the platter of salt.

"Pick up the chalice and hold it to your heart. In the chalice the elixir of life is contained. The water which is two-thirds of the planet as well as our bodies. The wine which is the nectar from the fruit of the vine. When you drink of the water and wine you drink of the divine. You are divine.

"As you sip the elixir allow yourself to commune with your own divinity and that of all life."

Lisa's head bowed. I knew she was looking within the chalice. Her mind no longer functioning in an analytical way. She was opening and merging with the energy of the ceremony. She was giving way to the female energy. She sipped the liquid, holding it in her mouth before swallowing. She brought the chalice back to her heart before returning it to the altar.

"Look at your altar, Lisa. See all the symbols which rest upon it. Look at the green plant and merge with it. Become. You are about to bless yourself, Lisa. This is a very important step of your healing. Feel this

expression for a moment. You may close your eyes if you wish."

In the silence I lit the charcoal on which I would place a special blend of herbs I had prepared for the ceremony. When a few minutes of silence had passed I placed a pinch of the herbal mixture on the charcoal. Immediately the sense of smell was aroused.

"Now we awaken the mind by usage of smell. Our sense of smell causes many reactions within us. We are either repulsed or tantalized. The mind immediately awakens and processes the smell, and then acts upon it by prompting an emotion into being.

"Take the matches in front of you and light the two candles. As you do so become aware of the increase in light around you and your altar."

Slowly she struck the match and applied it to the first taper on the left. After the wick took flame she picked up the taper and lit the right candle. I watched the back of her head turn from side to side as she took in the light.

"With the salt we acknowledged the element of Earth. With the wine and water we acknowledged the element of Water. With the incense we acknowledged the element of Air, and like wise with the flame we acknowledged the element of Fire.

"We now have the powers of the four directions surrounding us, and are ready to begin the ceremony."

I pushed the "play" button on the tape recorder next to me. The beautiful harp music of Anne Williams, Summer Rose crept into the room.

"Close your eyes and breathe within. Know that you are in a space that is made sacred by your essence. Now is the time of your divinity. Listen to the melodies dance around your head and heart. Join this dance." I left Lisa to her dance for a few minutes.

"With the first two fingers of your right hand dip them into the chalice of water/wine and touch them to your forehead. Of the earth you are made. She is your mother. Address now that connection by saying `Bless me Mother for I am your child.'"

I could hear Lisa speak the blessing.

"The third eye is the door-way into the realm of spirit. You have just acknowledged your own spirit and the place where your life-spark flows in this physical body. Breathe this truth."

"Dip your fingers again and touch them to your eyes and say, 'Bless my eyes to see your ways.' You are now ready to look at your life-path and see *if it is life-oriented or not. You are ready now to receive your vision and to see the truth in all situations. No longer will you be blind to your spirit; to your essence. Look in truth and see the path before you.*

"Again dip your fingers, but this time touch them to your nose. Now say, `Bless my nose that I may smell your essence.' Mind is stimulated by scent, and scent in turn stimulates the inner mind. We must learn to "smell-out" a situation and know that our smelling is alert. We must smell the essence of female, the essence of Mother Earth and come to know the different scents as truth and a part of what and who we are."

I placed a lavender bud on the charcoal. "Smell the fragrance of female, of nature. Of earth, of life and let the scent reawaken your subconscious mind."

I closed my eyes and allowed the molecules of the lavender bud to travel up my nostrils. How often we take smell for granted it, I thought to myself. We have learned to cover up all natural smells with synthetics instead of using the scents of nature.

The scent of lavender brought scenes of summer days to mind. The sun dancing among the stalks of buds popping up above the olive green filigree leaves and stems of the bush. Yellow butterflies darting here and there. Yes, the scent of nature could transform us.

I opened my eyes and focused on Lisa's back. Her breathing showed me she was lost deep within her own mind. The lightness of her energy had begun to shine around her. For the first time in weeks her aura was a constant glow of golden-white light.

"Dip your fingers in the chalice and anoint your lips. Say, `Bless my lips to speak of you.' All reality begins with thought. It is the mouth which sends forth the vibration of the thought to become manifested in the physical.

"The word is powerful. Sound is constant and vibration never stops. We bless our mouth so that we might think before we speak. We have a real responsibility in speaking only truth, and sending forth the vibration of the positive.

"Remember that it is the word that transforms. We touch the mind with words. We influence each other with words. Words become ritual, they are magic. They transform.

"If you speak in a positive manner about your female, then you are creating a positive force field around you which becomes a support system.

In turn your positive word of female touches the minds of others and helps them to begin perceiving first, and then speaking about the attributes of the female.

"Now that you have blessed your mouth dip your fingers in and touch your breasts. Focus on your breasts for a moment for they are a source of strength and beauty. From your breasts comes the nourishment of new life.

"The breasts are part of Women's Mysteries because they are a source of life nourishment. Feel this divinity. You nourish. This is the place from where your nourishment came as a new babe. You are part of the Female Source that has power to give.

"Now say, 'Bless my breasts formed in strength and beauty.' Know right now that Womanhood is this strength and beauty combined. To be strong is to be beautiful. You are being strong by taking responsibility for your female. In taking responsibility for your female you become beautiful because you are allowing your true essence to grow powerful and shine."

I could see a sob shake Lisa's body. In blessing herself, in accepting her female she was being born. She was awakening. She was becoming. It is sacred watching a woman shed an armour and reveal her spirit.

"Dip your fingers in and touch your womb and say, 'Bless my womb that brings forth life.' Now you acknowledge the Divine Female that you are. This is the place of mystery. This is the portal in your body from where life births.

"As a woman you have the choice to birth, or not. That is your divine right. Never let any one take that right from you.

"All people are born through women. You are a woman. This is your sacred mark. Rejoice in this Source of Life. Rejoice in the connection with the creative energies of the universe. Know that biologically you are superior to the male.

"Know that because of this truth you can live peacefully among the sexes, feeling complete, feeling whole, with no need to prove that you are equal to man. You are woman. Man comes out of woman. This is truth. This is a fact. You never have to prove that!"

I watched Lisa's shoulders pick-up. Suddenly she sat very erect, very proud. She was hearing an old truth for the first time. She was ready to understand just what being a woman was all about. She was part of the creative source of the universal life. She could create. She was divine. She was sacred.

"For the last time dip your fingers in the chalice and touch your feet saying, 'Bless my feet to walk the Beauty Path.'

"You have just accepted your Divine Power. You know that you think first and your feet will follow. You know that you think first and the word creates. So now is the time to be conscious of your path. You must use all your awareness now to journey down the path of truth and life.

"You are not powerless any more. Walking your path is an act of power.

"Lisa close your eyes now, and allow this experience to become fully integrated within your heart, within your mind, within your power center. Think about the way you have been living your life. Thank yourself for having the courage to perform this self-blessing. You are surrounded by Spirit Keepers who will help you on your path."

The flickering candle danced on the four walls of the room. Gentle harp strings unfolded with the woven echoing of a woman's voice. An auburn headed woman wrapped in a red silk kimono sat at the far end of the room. Magic was in the air.

The energy of the female had been invoked and was filling every inch of space, including our bodies, within the room. I felt my own body surrender to the wonderful nourishment rising from the earth. I began to dance with my arms as I sat behind Lisa. Slowly, and elegantly they lifted in the air above my head. Their shadows danced on the walls with the candle light.

In the quiet beneath the soft music I could hear the gentle sobbing of Lisa. My own heart burst open, silent tears slipped down my cheeks. I was so blessed. The Mother spoke through me; I was able to help sisters re-claim their power.

As the harp strings vibrated into the distance, and only the flickering of the candle light danced upon the walls, did I dare break the spell which had been woven around us.

"Rise to your feet Woman. Stand balanced and strong. Feel the blending of knowledge, experience the wisdom within you. Allow energies to well-up within you, flow through you.

"Shine now. Shine and light up the whole room. When you are ready thank your Divine self for attending. Thank the Spirit Keepers. Thank Mother Earth. Thank the female force of life.

"Then extinguish the candles thanking all the elements for attending. Your self-blessing ceremony has ended."

I watched Lisa stand and rock back and forth - left to right, right to left. I could hear her silent thanks ring out into the room. I could feel her release each energy, and the energy withdraw back into the spirit realm.

When only Lisa and her new born energy stood before me she bent over and blew out both flames. As she turned to face me I stood.

Tears stained her face, her lips curving into the most beautiful smile I'd ever seen her wear. She rushed into my arms, and then, thanked me...

RELIGION AND THE FEAR OF GOD

If you are a woman who grew up in a household that was part of an orthodox religion you have been conditioned to believe you are inferior to man, that you are evil, and from day one the fear of God has been placed in your heart.

You are constantly reminded that you are a sinner, and repent now, or burn in hell for all eternity.

God becomes a horrible entity who only wants to punish and harm his so-called children of earth.

If your views on life, religion, and God ever expanded and you asked questions beyond what the church taught, you were in league with the devil, and once again fear was etched deep into your spirit.

It has become increasingly easy to overcome the fear of God as we are intellectually and consciously awakening today.

We have but to stop and think about the child who was brainwashed with all this negative propaganda and ask ourselves some basic questions.

l. What is your image of God?

Is he a white, bearded man who sits on a throne in heaven looking down upon his supposed creation? If so, this is the left-over of childhood. What is God really?

God is the male, or masculine energy which exists in our present day world. It is the polarity/opposite of the co-existing female energy.

God is the aspect of divinity which generates action in the physical. Within its own completeness there is a duality, issuing forth a positive energy or a negative one. "God Bless", is the invocation of the positive energy which we have come to know as protective and guiding. "God damn," is the invocation of the negative energy which we have come to know as destructive and fearful.

For so long the negative energy has been invoked by the heads of his "supposed" church. Through the priests, who claim to be pious followers and believers of God, they continually use his negative aspect to gain control over the people; elevate their position within society to the highest seats. They have become wealthy and cared-for by and at the expense of the people.

They have rigorously claimed their way is the one and only, and in the past have gone so far as to completely annihilate any other existing paths of truth in the most blood-curdling and animalistic manners.

Their belief in their other God, Satan, has aided them in performing masochistic acts against other human-beings. In doing so they say it is the "will of God." In reality, it was the will of their God, God Satan. Not God the heavenly father, the co-existing duality of life.

As a woman of spirit it is time to meet God. God the heavenly father, the male energy, the duality of female, the life-giving energy.

If you chose to place an image on this divine energy then chose one that is personal; one which has sacred meaning to you. Remember that the God energy has many aspects and can be worked with in many different ways.

It is time to stop feeding the God-image the church uses, or man uses, and feed the God energy of your heart in the most intimate, and female way you can. Give to God the male image, the male aspects you know as truly divine, truly a positive. Allow this new image of God, the heart God, to live peacefully within you from this day forward.

2. What is your image of Satan/the devil?

If you conjure up in your mind a image of a hedonistic being with horns, forked tail and tongue, clawed fingers, the color red, standing amidst flames, then ask yourself are you looking at this from your woman power or the memory of child?

Satan, or the devil, in reality is the monster of the mind. The scare tactic the priests of the church thought up to force the people into submission to gain control. Therefore, the devil is the evoked negative aspect of God the almighty.

In our past it is primarily the women who have been associated with the devil according to the priests of the church. Think about that. The women are said to be fornicators with this being. That they worshipped and believed in this being. That they had their own religion that centered around this being who so boldly paraded around naked covered with "red" skin, wearing a crown of horns on its head.

Dr. Margaret Murry summoned up the above dilemma in one profound sentence, when she wrote: "The God of the old religion becomes the devil of the new."[12]

I do not deny that there exists today a very negative energy that can be invoked by calling forth the devil, or Satan. Man has created it and given it life. It dwells within the recesses of our minds. We as women have the ability to not add our energy to this entity, but to put it to rest. We must teach our children the truth about this male God, and we must not give life to it within our own being.

The devil, or Satan, does not exist for us. Take responsibility and shut the door to this male foolishness. "There is no devil. There is no Satan. I do not believe in this entity. Therefore, I will not, and do not give life to it."

3. What is your image of Jesus Christ?

Whether you believe in Jesus, the man; son of God, or in Christ as consciousness we can all learn valuable lessons from the teachings of Jesus Christ.

Christ is the heart path. It is pure love. It is acceptance and understanding. It is compassion and tenderness. It is knowing right from wrong. It is total balance, total equality. It is perfection.

Christ is the positive personification of God. The light, the guider, the protector. The care-taker of the children on Mother Earth. From the Virgin Mother he was born. He was the example of female/male balance. He was the example of truth.

Jesus Christ born by a Virgin; the son of God. Did he become a consort to the Goddess (Mary Magdalini)? Was he a sacrificial king (the crucifixion)? Was he a man who supported the Goddess religion in a pure way (12 women apostles)? A man who understood the very principles of the female/male balance within the body as well as life on earth, and so, in understanding did he take this message to the people?

Women have always accepted Christ for what he was, allowing his light to shine. Men have not always seen the role-model he represents because his teachings have been perverted by his own apostles. The best example is that of Paul. Paul, whose writings influence the new testament, hated women, yet Christ showed their equality. Even his own apostles, failed to see the full message of Christ.

Was Jesus Christ's message an attempt at bridging the gap between male and female? Food for thought.

It is time for women to teach the heart path. Men have failed at understanding these most basic concepts of life. Perhaps, one of the messages Christ was trying to portray was "man, let the woman teach you my path; the path of the heart."

4. What is your image of the Virgin Mary?

Is she unimportant? Just the mother who gave birth to Jesus? Don't feel bad if you answered yes to both of these questions. For that is what the orthodox religions teach. She is just a character in the background. Don't pay too much attention to her, nor give her much power.

Ah, Virgin Mary; the Holy Mother who gives birth to the son of God. From woman all are born; male and female alike.

Mary was a Priestess of the temple of the Goddess. She was a Virgin; unmarried; performing all acts of life for the Mother. Virgin birth; a child born by a Priestess of the Great Goddess. That is one theory. However, Mary is simply the personification of the Goddess and her son. The "pagan's" would not adhere completely to the "new religion" and so the Goddess was brought in the picture as simply a woman who gave birth to the son of God but was not deemed as a necessary or important part of the bigger picture. It is time to recognize this new mythology and accept it for what it is; no longer being ruled by it.

As a woman, who is taking her power, it is time to understand the conditionings of child, and re-claim your mental and emotional bodies. It is time to heal the pains of child, and learn the lessons already provided for your journey on the woman spirit path. It is time to understand that women have been denied in today's religions. This fact has only been spotlighted in the last fifteen years thanks to the Seattle Coalition on Women and Religion who extracted this following statement from the Church Council.

A STATEMENT OF CONFESSION

"When we as the church begin to address the issue of women and religion, we must begin with an act of confession. We have found ourselves

to be in a position of conforming to the cultures, attitudes, and system of male dominance rather than seeking to transform them. Moveover, we have supported male dominance within the church itself, denying to women justice in receiving recognition and opportunity to participate as whole persons within the community of faith. As a result, we tend to read and interpret the Bible selectively, emphasizing what supports our biases."[13]

We are no longer victims. We are healers, and care-takers of our own spirit. It is time for us to love ourselves, to honor ourselves, and to know and become the sacredness that we are.

It is time to re-claim the female energy and embrace the divinity of it; to become Goddesses who walk on this great Mother body. It is time for us to nurture each other; to help show mankind the spirit path once more. It is time to walk in balance; male and female alike.

Let us join hands as sisters and unite our energy. Form this bond out of love with the purpose of healing all relations who walk beside you. Form this bond with the focus of achieving true balance.

...The new calender year had birthed. It was a day full of white, fluffy clouds and quiet. Thora had traveled down from Santa Barbara. We sat talking in my living room sipping mugs of steaming coffee. We were waiting for my apprentices to arrive. We would perform a ceremony today; one which would direct the energies for the next solar cycle towards self-healing and divine forgiveness.

They soon arrived dressed in flowing skirts with pastel shawls draped around their hips. Introductions were made, hugs and kisses exchanged, then off to the back-bay we headed.

It was a lovely walk. The streets were deserted. The residents of the neighborhood lounging indoors; taking full advantage of the first day of the new year. Soon our feet were raising small clouds of dust as we tread the path which cut down to the grove of pampas grass next to the natural harbor.

Once within our circle of bush, we established where center would be and staked out the quarters. Candles were lit and placed in each spot with items of correspondence. We were ready to begin ceremony.

We came into the center and joined hands. Together we closed our eyes and breathed deep grounding our roots into Mother Earth. Opening, our branches rose to the universe providing a direct line for the light energy to flow down into our being.

We allowed our own centeredness to release and flow around the center through each of us until the connection was achieved. Lazily, we opened our eyes allowing our focus to adjust.

Each of us chose a quarter. Turning to face the direction we began to call them in. Gail stood in the east, Thora in the south, Lisa in the west and I filled in the north. After the elements were acknowledged we turned back to center where I called the Mother.

We chanted the traditional Charge of the Star Goddess followed by the "I Am" chant.

Thora, with her sufi background, taught us a chant. Two simple words: "Ah-Shim, Vou-Hu", which translates into "God above, God within". We began acknowledging the God energy of the heavens by raising our hands to the sky, then lowering them to our own heart center to acknowledge the God force within.

After repeating this movement four times we brought the focus and movement to the center of our circle acknowledging the God force within our ceremony. We chanted and moved allowing the energy to flow; a sense of peace and unity settling around us. When we finished our hands covered our hearts. We were high.

I asked Thora if she would lead us for the divine forgiveness. She taught us another sufi chant. As our voices rose into the new year day our minds held images of those people who had hurt us in one way or another.

In our own way we found the energy of forgiveness flowing, erasing the painful memories. Releasing the forgiveness we sent it into the heavens to be carried away to those people we had privately thought of.

The energy shifted to heal our hearts and minds, to forgive ourselves. We became instruments of divine forgiveness.

With our focus on Mother Earth we circled moon-wise chanting a healing song.

> *"The earth is our Mother,*
> *we must take care of her.*
> *The earth is our Mother,*
> *we must take care of her.*
>
> *"Hey, nawa, Ho nawa, Hey na na*
> *Hey, nawa, Ho nawa, Hey na na.*

"Her sacred ground we walk upon,
with every step we take.
Her sacred ground we walk upon,
with every step we take."[14]

It felt ancient to dance round and round shaking our rattles, first to the sky, and then to the earth. Raising our hands above our heads to turn first clock-wise in a circle, then unwind moon-wise. We became absorbed in the dance. Each of us lost in our own special prayers of healing for this great body we live on.

As I moved with the others I found my own focus going to the great fault-lines running up and down California. It was important to send my energy there. So many people had started imagining a larger-than-life earthquake devastating California. I felt in my heart it wasn't a necessary event, but through the focused energy of the doomsday fanatics the event could manifest.

Slowly, the dance came to a halt. The four of us stood with eyes closed. The energy raised landed softly upon the Mother.

We joined hands, ready to turn the healing onto ourselves. Tenderly we began singing.

"I am a circle, I am healing you.
You are a circle, you are healing me.

"Unite us, be as one.
Unite us, be as one."[15]

Our bodies swayed back and forth with the gentle vibrations. We stood that way, eyes closed, bodies swaying, hands joined for many cycles of the song. Then quietly, one by one, we took turns standing in the center.

When my turn came and I stood in the center all healing was directed to me. I closed my eyes receiving the love around me. Their voices and the soothing touch of their hands caressed my body.

It felt as if thousands of hands were touching me. A cool one resting over my third eye. Warmth laying over my heart. Tension eased out of my neck. Nurturance placed over my womb. All weariness was brushed out of my feet, and a friend held my hand in hers eventually stroking my palm.

My back was stroked, my arms were touched, the length of my legs were smoothed over by the gentle, healing touch of a being full of love, life, divine forgiveness, and a healing grace greater than any I had ever felt.

As the touching hands withdrew one by one, the memory still lingered over my body. I felt light pouring in through my crown and Mother Earth's rich support naturally flowing in through the soles of my feet. Very, very slowly I opened my eyes. Smiles greeted me. I joined the circle.

Once more we held hands and sang the song over and over and over. Our bodies swaying. Our minds filled with divine forgiveness. Our hearts flowing with healing. Our energy was a glowing ball of pure love. We ended the healing with a giant group hug and kisses planted on cheeks, lips, noses and shoulders.

Giggling we broke the trance we had fallen into and went back to our quarters. I thanked the Mother for her divine presence. Thora thanked the God for his divine strength. Lisa and Gail thanked life for our divine life.

We individually thanked the energy of the elements and opened circle. Our rite had ended. We were ready to face the new solar year...

CHAPTER IV

THE GODDESS

Who is the Goddess? What is she? This is a question many people are asking today. She is many things. She is ancient and young. She is serious and playful. She is the creative life force which flows through all women. She is the womb.

The Goddess is the female aspect of God. God is the male aspect of Goddess. Both, are the polarities of the Eternal One, the Great Spirit, the Divine Life Force, the Creative Energy of Physical Manifestations.

The Goddess is the Great Wisdom referred to in the Judeo-Christian Bible.[16]

[13] Happy is the man that findeth Wisdom, and the man that getteth understanding.

[14] For the merchandise of it is better than the merchandise of silver, and the gain greater thereof than fine gold.

[15] She is more precious than rubies; and all the things thou canst desire are not to be compared unto her.

[16] Length of days is in her right hand; and in her left riches and honor.

[17] Her ways are ways of pleasantness, and all her paths are peace.
[18] She is a tree of life to them that lay hold upon her; and happy is everyone that retaineth Her. *Proverbs 3:13-18*

As a woman, to come to know the Goddess is an act of liberation; of freeing the female soul. For the Goddess is the power of woman.

Her aspects in life are portrayed through the phases of the moon. The silver crescent Maiden, the full and swollen Mother, the dark and mysterious Crone.

The virtuoso of myth interpretation, Joseph Campbell,[17] tells us, "She is incarnate in every woman." As a woman's body waxes and wanes with her monthly mensus she does indeed imitate the Triple Goddess, the moon.

The ancient religion of the Goddess still lives today. Remnants of it are found throughout the world as ancient ruins are uncovered by archaeologists. Scholastic writings based on its existence, and importance line the bookshelves.

The oldest artifacts in the history of the world unearthed throughout Europe and Asia, and from Spain to Russia, carbon-dated about 25,000 B.C., are figurines of the fertility aspect of the Goddess, the Paleolithic Venus.[18] Ancient Goddess Shrines throughout Europe, Turkey and Greece still stand today.

Archaeologists have shown the height of the Goddess worship was in the Neolithic communities about 7,000 B.C., and the overthrow of the ancient religion was somewhere between 1800 and 1550 B.C., the time of Abraham.[19] The final suppression of the old religion was not until the time of the Christian emperors of Rome and Byzantine in about 500 A.D. It was at this time the last of the Goddess temples were closed down [20] and the old religion went underground.

Though the Goddess religions existence went underground, for thousands of years, due to religious and political uprisings, today it is resurfacing. Men and woman alike are experiencing the golden value of coming face-to-face with the Goddess. Life becomes holier and love becomes abundant. Awareness of our responsibility to our planet – Mother Earth, is re-established and peace, world peace, is sought.

Through the resurgence of Goddess awareness, we are traveling down a path which has brought a semi-state of balance back to the souls of men. Women become stronger in their own life force, and men are able to open their hearts.

Matriarchy-Patriarchy: neither of these systems have entirely worked. The blending of the two will create a new way, a more peaceful way. Mind, body and soul will re-align and the polarities of the Eternal One will flow through the life creation once more. Balance. Conscious balance. Spiritual balance.

The Goddess religion, or awareness is not about woman's oppression. Unfortunately, to a great deal, many of the current books available today reek of the resurgence of the Goddess from this perspective. A very feminist approach has been taken. As a result, the Goddess energy is being redirected into our consciousness from an aggressive, oppressive and hostile point of view.

While women are standing up and saying, "Look, here is my origin. Here is my 'God'. This is the life force that flows through me, and I am willing to embrace it.", there is also a counter-attack coming from women who are saying, "Fuck you, god-damned men. You are the ones that stripped women of their rights. You annihilated our religion by brutally massacring our female ancestors who peacefully and harmoniously walked their path by glorifying the creative, nurturing life force - the Goddess. How dare you!"

What is wrong with that? What's wrong with that approach, you may repeat in your mind. How does one answer that question?

As I sat and dwelled on the answer to this question, I was taken back in memory to a beautiful autumn day.

...I sat on the south rim of the Grand Canyon looking down into the depths; an opening in the Mother Earth. It was late afternoon, and the sun-rays slanted across the desert terrain as they drifted on the west horizon down to meet the land.

It was peaceful. Scattered about the large dirt parking lot were a few other cars, the sight-seers scattered around the rim of the Grand Canyon. Off to one side sat a row of thatched roof huts. The huts containing the Navajo and their turquoise jewelry and wares.

Time stood still out here in the mid-west where the Cowboys and

Indians still fought over the land. Each trying to survive among the elements. Each trying to keep alive an essential lifestyle their spirit required.

Cowboys and Indians. How many of those movies had we seen while growing up? Movies where Burt Lancaster, red-skinned and handsome, grunted or shoved his beautiful squaw in silence across the great basin. Or Dustin Hoffman growing old before our very eyes as he struggled through the Little Bighorn massacre of Custer.

"I'll be the Cowboy, and you be the Indian," we would tell each other. My brother would dress-up in his hip holster and cowboy hat. I would wrap something around my head and begin the war cries. I became the warrior squaw and was the one always killed in the end.

I thought of the Native Americans and their struggles with the new race of men that came to the Americas. Why was it, I thought to myself, that all peaceful, earth-loving people are slaughtered? Is it simply the animalistic characteristics of man which take over when the hunger for power controls the mind? The mind - the ego; our greatest enemy.

Yes, time stood still while I sat there looking out across the land which lay perfect and unreal. A manifestation beyond my conception.

Who dreamed this great beauty up, was my question. And then I saw the answer right there before my eyes. The sun shifted a little lower and shadows filled in the spots the sun-rays could no longer reach.

Blackbirds suddenly lifted up from some hidden spot below. A field mouse crept out from under the scrub sage bush I was standing behind. Blue. Shades of blue radiated up from the vast opening. Rose washed over the sky melting down to join the blue.

It was everywhere. Goddess and God. They danced and joined everywhere. They filled in the spaces the other could not at that particular point of the dance. Yet, always they rejoined; merging their beauty. Female and male.

Both aspects of life would always exist. If we wanted to find supreme balance, we have but to stop and watch the sunset; the dance of the two energies. For within the full spectrum of their dance are qualities of beauty and strength, honor and humility, mirth and reverence. One does not overpower the other. They simply, and naturally flow; blending together where they come to meet. Otherwise, in the places were they stand alone, they are a strength and a completeness within themselves...

No, the importance of the Goddess is not about how oppressed women have been, and still are because of their own ignorant stubbornness at perpetuating that attitude. The real importance is to rise up with the Goddess energy and become a strength and a completeness within ourselves. Not to try to over-power the male and his connection with God, but simply and naturally to flow; blending together when we meet.

Respect and acceptance. We cannot undo the past. Nor can we continue to blame other people for what happened in the past, especially before this life. Now is the time to show respect and acceptance, and in our own strong and beautiful way to become, once more, our part of creation – the female energy, the Goddess.

Consciously, we have come to a state where the blending of the two is now possible. And, if we bring back the Goddess in such a hostile and attacking manner towards the male population, who can blame them if they reject us and Her.

No more blame. No more attack. We have evolved as a whole to the point where we are understanding that victory and honor does not have to be accomplished over the shedding of blood, but through the wisdom of understanding. Opening the heart and joining the mind with it. And in the end simply accepting another person`s ways and respecting their spirit enough to allow them their own path.

CHAPTER V

BONDING

Truth or dare. Bonding is about honesty. Allowing yourself to be vulnerable with other women. Lowering the walls which separate us. Putting aside the judgement and jealousy. Opening the heart, connecting the mind, and joining the power centers.

...*"Let's play truth or dare," I said to Gail and Lisa as they sat before me in the flickering candle light. They smiled nodding their heads. Lisa looked at Gail.*

"Oh, boy," she said. "Here we go. You can tell this is going to be a good one."

They had learned to read the signs of my mischevious nature. The nature which always, in the end, hit them with power having such an impact in their hearts that they walked away with new understanding.

"We lack the ethics of communication." They glanced at each other; puzzeled expressions written all over their faces. "No, not just us," I explained. "But society as a whole."

We sat with our backs together, listening to the night. Quiet was all around us. For once the neighborhood kids were no where to be found. We centered ourselves, then allowed the energy to travel round the circle connecting us. Tonight we were going to become vulnerable. I could feel their nervousness; silently hoping the evenings work would be a success.

"There are two ways of speaking the truth," I began. "One way is a blatant accusation. The second is speaking only about how you are feeling without relating to the other person the truth of the matter.

"Often we don't tell the other person the truth because you wouldn't 'dare' be that honest with anyone. Tonight we shall learn the difference between the two, and combine them. We will learn to speak open and honestly in the most positive way, for both people involved."

Silence hugged us. I allowed the women to absorb what I said.

"Let us begin with `dare'. This is a direct accusation. Normally, when you give a `dare' the person you are directing it to becomes defensive. We are going to speak a `dare' to each other. Lisa, I will begin by giving you a `dare', then you will give Gail one, and Gail, you will give me a `dare'.

"When it is your turn to speak, think about the `dare'. Do not begin to speak until you are clear. If you are receiving the `dare' then you must listen and not interrupt. Listening is also a part of communication. Listening to the other person and hearing the full scope of what they are saying before speaking or interrupting.

"Okay, close your eyes for a moment. Breath easy. Relax. I will begin when I am ready."

This always proves to be a very valuable lesson on bonding as well as communication because truths are revealed and issues dealt with. I began by telling Lisa she had a problem letting go of her past, continually playing the victim, and because of that she was unable to make progress in being present and in the moment.

Lisa told Gail about her weight problem, that it was a result of her insecurities. Gail finished the circle by telling me I brought my personal life into the group.

Each one of us listened to the `dare' quietly. There was a slight tension in the air and between us when we finished. I instructed the women to close their eyes and relax. After a few moments of quiet we turned and faced each other.

Looking into each others eyes I asked how they had felt giving as well as receiving a `dare'.

"I was nervous," Lisa began. "When you began to speak, but after I heard your dare, and really listened to what you were saying, I realized it

was a truth. But, the manner in which it was given, as a `dare', did make me defensive. My little girl immediately came up and thought `but, Kisma, you don't understand'."

All three of us nodded agreement. It seems that when you receive a `dare' it feels as if the other person does not understand what you are going through, and because of that, arguments can break-out. The rule: we had to be silent and receive the `dare' prevented an argument from arising.

Lisa continued. "When it was my turn to give Gail a `dare' I suddenly felt short of breath. I knew I would be hurting her. Yet, I went ahead and spoke the `dare'." Again, we all had experienced the same reaction.

Giving a blatant `dare' to another person is a focused act of hurting. Arguments begin out of self-defence, then a wounding match or an `who can out dare the other person' competition begins.

"Now that you delivered a `dare' not having to look the person in the eye we are going to do the same excercise. This time facing each other."

Stiffly the women shifted their positions. I laughed and brought their attention back to the safe enviornment we were in and reminded them that this was only an excercise.

We began delivering the `dare' the opposite direction. I told Gail that sometimes she allowed her focus to wander, and did not apply herself to learning the required information I assigned. I felt is was a result of her fear of failure.

Gail told Lisa she kept repeating patterns by making more out of a situation by comparing it to the past. Lisa told me she felt I got impatient with her when she didn't learn the information I assigned.

Again, we shared our emotions. All agreed it was much harder to look the person in the eye and speak. The same feelings were present on the receiving end. It just wasn't easy to receive a `dare' no matter how truthful it was. We agreed it was definately a hateful act to deliver a `dare'.

We regrouped in the center, our backs together, and released the `dare' excersise. We were moving on to the `truth' portion.

"The same rules apply when delivering, or receiving a `truth'," I informed them. "When you give your `truth' it should be something the person does that isn't necessarily a negative, but a situation you respond negatively to. I will start with Gail. This time we will face each other. `Truths' are easier to deliver because it is a form of self-indulgence, and normally takes on a whining characteristic.

"Okay, lets relax a moment, then turn and face each other."

When we turned and faced each other there were smiles of nervousness. 'Truths' were just as difficult to deliver because now we would hear about something we did which annoyed another person. Of course, the accusation would still be there, just in an under-handed way.

"Gail," I began after having allowed the 'truth' to enter my mind. "I feel really unappreciated when you forget to do things we have discussed and agreed on. It makes we wonder whether or not I am wasting my time."

Gail allowed this to be absorbed. She took a moment of silence, followed by a deep breath, then turned to Lisa. "Lisa, I feel you hold things in and don't share them. This creates a distance and I feel hurt, like you keep your personal life from me."

Lisa nodded, she heard what Gail was saying. Then she turned to face me. "Kisma, I sometimes feel insecure when I'm around you because I think you know everything already, and that makes me hesitant about sharing any information."

The breathing resumed its normal rhythm. We discussed the experiment. We agreed we did not feel as defensive when receiving a 'truth', but there was also a sense of not having received the full scope of the 'truth'.

Delivering the 'truth' was a lot easier than a 'dare' because you weren't directly accusing the person of a particular thing. Instead you were softening the edges, turning the problem around and assuming responsibility for your reaction.

We agreed 'truths' were a much better manner in which to approach another person. However, it still lacked total communication, which brought us to the next part of the experiement - combining the two.

Once again we put our backs together to feel the solidness of each other. I continued.

"Truth or dare. We must learn to apply the same rules. If you are delivering a 'truth or dare' to a person who has no conception of the ethics of communication you may not be able to get in the full 'truth or dare'. Especially, not if you start out with a 'dare'. So, you must always start out with a 'truth', and hope this person will listen to the full scope of what you need to say.

"As someone who has experienced a lesson in 'truth or dare', you must now begin applying the concept of listening when you are approached by someone whether they are delivering a 'truth' or a 'dare'. You must listen

no matter how hard it is for you to keep the mouth shut. It is our responsibility to begin teaching.

"How do we best teach? By being an example of that which we are teaching." The girls nodded they understood.

"Okay, so in delivering a 'truth or dare', we are choosing to deliver the total truth, or the total picture to another person. Remember this total truth or picture is only from our perspective. Clarify that from the beginning.

"I will begin with Lisa. Remember do not deliver your 'truth or dare' until you are clear on what it is you need to say."

I drew a complete blank as I turned to look at Lisa. I had to sit there a few moments and allow my mind to quiet. Finally, it jumped up. I turned to her and smiled. This one was going to be hard for me.

"Lisa, I need to share this with you because it is something that happened between us a few months ago and, I guess, I haven't been able to let it go." I took a breath and looked at her. She was ready to receive. She smiled and nodded.

"I was hurt when you never responded back about becoming roommates. I felt you were inconsiderate. You voiced that you needed to move out. I needed a roommate, so I offered. You said you would let me know in a week. But, you never brought the subject up again.

"I understand, Lisa. It would be hard living with me since you are my apprentice. I guess I just think of that situation differently. I have always been someone who would jump at the chance of becoming a 'true' apprentice and living with my teacher. I guess I was offended that you didn't perceive the situation in that manner.

"I also felt it was a reflection of your real commitment towards learning the craft. I also felt it was a statement of how you really value me as your teacher."

Silence. She kept her gaze down. I could tell this one had also been in the back of her mind. A few minutes passed before she was able to turn and face Gail.

"Gail, I really get annoyed with you when you won't allow your inner voice, your wisdom to speak out. You have so much more inside of you than you are willing to admit. I realize you don't speak out because you are insecure about it. Believe me I can relate to where you're coming from. I'm going through some of the same feelings. But Gail, you have to overcome that fear, and just do it."

Gail received this information willingly. It was an affirmation for her. In silence she sat there nodding her head. She turned to me, smiled nervously, adjusting her body to face me.

"Kisma, I feel under a lot of pressure from you right now. I know you feel unappreciated. Your path is one of helping and teaching people. You are under a lot of pressure right now with a lot of people coming to you for their own needs. You are going through a lot of your own personal stuff and it seems as if all your doing is giving, and no one is returning the energy back.

"Kisma, you need to know we do value you. You are important. You need to accept your path and do the work that you've committed yourself to doing, and above all else, realize your validity."

I sat there for a moment allowing her words to sink in. Boy, was that the truth. I smiled at her, said "thank you".

Delivering a "truth or dare" is very positive as well as helpful to another. It is not an attack, it does not make anyone defensive. Instead it mixes the bitter with the sweet, shedding light on all angles. It portrayes compassion and friendship.

Communication is an act of sharing; a need to understand a situation or be understood. Communicating honestly is possible. It requires the combination of wisdom and knowledge. The knowledge of what to say and the wisdom of how to say it.

"Truth or dare" is that combination.

We hugged each other after discussing the personal issues, and for the first time in the nine months we had been working together felt really tight.

We closed the evening by just sitting and holding hands; sharing the new found closeness; the honesty which had been shared; the insights into our own natures. Each of us had received valuable tools to apply toward the betterment of our own development.

That evening we parted knowing that we had dared to share truths that some people never have the courage to do in a life time...

Ethics of communication is something everyone should be taught in school. We would not only learn positive, constructive ways to communicate, we would also learn how to resolve conflicts together instead of perpetuating the "divide and conquer" modus-operandi of today's society.

When we learn to resolve conflicts together we create harmony within our relationships, and promote integrity within ourselves.

Most of us have learned to either be a victim or a rescuer, instead of an equal participant in life. We resume these roles creating dissension in our relationships creating miscommunication. Our perceptions of life often become unrealistic and negative.

Being a rescuer always leads to becoming a persecuter. Communications that deal with being a rescuer usually occur in the following common situations:

1. Any situation in which you do something that you don't want to do in a relationship with another person.

2. When, in any joint activity, you put in more effort or more interest than the other person.

3. Not asking for what you want; perhaps because you are afraid of the other person's reaction.

4. Not talking straight about your feelings.

5. The situation of doing something for another person without being asked, or without you first having asked them if you can help.

There is a Big and little rescuer. The Big rescuer doesn't expect to succeed. In fact, they expect to fail, and in failing become persecuted by the victim they originally try to rescue.

Because of their failure, the Big rescuer becomes a Big persecutor who turns on the victim and says, "I warned you", or the most common statement, "I told you so." This mostly occurs in a situation where the victim may have asked for help.

If the Big rescuer was not asked for help or they did not offer to help they become a victim upon failing by discounting their own feelings and abilities. Self-doubt is the number one cause of the victim mode.

A true, or little rescuer, is the person who has taken a career in civil service such as a lifeguard, fireman, nurse, police officer, doctor, counselor. They expect to rescue others and do. They expect success and succeed. They expect thank you's and gratification, and receive thank you's and gratification. They do not become the Big victim.

We must learn to let go of the hero attitude, and not try to rescue anyone uless we are qualified to do so. If in our daily living we are brought into a situation were we act from the heart helping another spirit re-build or re-pair their life, it must be done for that reason alone, to help another spirit, not for sense gratification.

There is a little persecutor as well as a little victim. The little persecutor is someone who consciously persecutes: religious fanatics, Hitler's, politicians, promoters of any situation flavored with the divide and conquer attitude such as those who perpetuated the Inquisitions.

The little victim is a victin in a truer sense as they have become oppressed by someone in an aggressive manner. In other words, someone who has been raped, mugged, and injured in some way as the result of an assault.

We must learn to shake off these Big Roles we assume and turn our rescue attempts on ourselves. The purpose of constructive self criticism is to educate and protect ourselves as well as to advance one's cause. It is the most empowering tool we can use.

If used properly, we can over come certain situations, emotions, and patterns of a most negative nature. A very simple example/tool to use is to ask yourself the following question, and answer it before opening your mouth or reacting to another person.

When I did (*observation of my action*), I caused (*effect of my action*) and from now on I will do (*action doing it better*) because of (*purpose*).[21]

When communicating with another person, "truth or dare" is a positive method to use. However, a form of constructive criticism to use with another person is found in the following. (Remember a golden rule to follow is: think out the situation you wish to communicate clearly before speaking about it.)

When you do (*observation*), I feel (*emotion*) and I want you to do (*action – want*), because of (*purpose what cause will it advance*).

We take for granted our communication skills. Because of this we continually communicate in a damaging manner. In taking responsibility for your communication skills you are actively putting a stop to gossip, back stabbing, miscommunication, and disharmony between you and others.

When you begin to put into effect this new commitment you will begin to notice how much deceit in communication has become integrated in almost every aspect of society. You will come to realize that most relationships, whether they be working or personal, lack true honesty, true communications. Suddenly, everywhere you turn you see the hidden agendas peeking out from behind words.

When you find yourself in the crossfire of two people turn the situation into a constructive sounding board rather than a gossip session. Tell the person who wants to complain or slander another, you will discuss the issue with them only if the next conversation they have on the subject is with the person they are complaining about.

Tell them that you will be a sounding board to set in order the issues which need to be settled; that you will not take sides, nor will you contribute to the negative emotions they are experiencing by gossiping.

Sometimes a miscommunication between two people needs a mediator to settle it. Once you have gained control over your own communication skills, sharpen them by offering to be a mediator.

Being a mediator is really quite simple. All you are doing is controlling a discussion by establishing guide-lines the two people agree to follow.

The basic guidelines are:

1. Each person has a full 15 minutes of uninterrupted time to speak. The speaking must be delivered either as "truth or dare" or constructive criticism.

2. There will be no name calling, or aggressive, physical behavior.

3. Both parties are seeking a resolution to the problem.

4. You (the mediator) will not take sides, will only speak if there is a stalemate, at which time you will simply reiterate what each person has been saying.

Sometimes a couple of sessions are required when you are dealing with people who have no conscious awareness of the amount of deceit they have been employing in their communications most, if not all, their life.

When mediating it is important to pay attention to any paranoid fantasies that may arise. When someone has a paranoid fantasy it means they are intuitively picking up on something. Rather than making assumptions, instruct the person having the fantasy to check it out with the other party. They can present it by using qualifing statement openings such as, *"I have this paranoid fantasy that you are jealous of, etc."* and then continue with the full truth of the fantasy.

The correct response to a paranoid fantasy is to validate a seed of truth, which means searching inside for the seed. In other words, both parties must examine this fantasy, not just the person having it.

All miscommunications can be resolved by using mediations. (Better, we all learn the correct tools to put an end to miscommunication.)

If conflict should evolve within a group, effecting two or more, it is important to take care of it upon the first outbreak. Mediation is the most efficent and personal manner to handle this situation, especially when only two members are involved. However, if the conflict includes more than two there is a Radical Therapy Mediation which a whole group can undergo.

The basic steps are as follow:

1. Make sure all those involved want a mediation, and find out which people do not want the mediation.

2. Exchange held resentments.

3. De-mystify paranoid fantasies/unclear feelings.

4. Discuss perceptions of the problem.

5. Look for and de-mystify the contradictions among the people involved. Have a self-conscious critical,and self-critical discussion of perceptions of the problem.

6. Figure out what people want to do about it; finding out what people want from each other.

7. Make contracts and work on them.

8. Get and give strokes (of love and appreciation) no matter what the outcome (should the group stay together or disband).

Though I have never personally gone through a Radical Therapy Mediation, I have witnessed the positive effect it had on a group. This group choose to disband, forming two separate groups. Because they used the above forum for conflict resolution they have been able to maintain a working relationship and often do work together on public events.

Unfortunately, I have been in a group where ego's were so large individuals refused to accept the fact there was a conflict within the group. The group refused to have a forum despite the urging of a few of us. As a result, the group completely disbanded within only a few short weeks. Many of the members left on very bad terms. In fact, many have never spoken since. That was five years ago.

If you are in a group and seeking a good set of guide-lines for communication the following list is most helpful.

ETHICS OF COMMUNICATION [22]

1. Personal agendas are valid; secret of purpose is unethical and anti-group. Secrecy of purpose creates dishonest/unethical communication.

2. Invalidating another person is an unethical means of advocating a point of view.

3. Seeking power over group direction by blocking the voices of others is non-consensual in intent and outcome.

4. It is the groups responsibility to make sure that no one person is alone though they may hold a singular view-point.

5. Empowerment of each member is the responsibility of all members.

6. Persons have a right to information that effects them.

7. Each member has an obligation to get/be/stay clear with other members; each person owes it to each other to do that clearing with her/him, and not by speaking it out with others.

8. The purpose of each individuals communication is to work toward agreement not to shape decissions in their own image.

9. There are times when it is valid for members to agree that what is said in the room, stays in the room. It is fair for the group to demand that some things be spoken about only as a group, not individually.

10. People know/notice when there is conflict, pain, or mistrust between/among members.

11. Every personal realtionship between members of a group effects the group, therefore may be personal but not always private.

12. The means is the ends. (Process is important. How a group works together will determine the value they have as a group.)

The surest way to establish a solid bond between individuals as well as a group is to follow a code of ethics, and to work on continually applying that code.

The only way we can truly bond with others is when we trust them. Trust comes from honesty. Honesty is based on communication.

The above skills I have provided is a place to start in developing communication skills. It is important as sisters to speak openly and honestly to each other. We must put an end to the gossip sessions, and back-stabbing reputation we have become notorius as having.

This new reputation placed on women regarding deceit and dishonesty in communication has been a result of our segregation. The segregation has resulted in jealousy and has developed fear between us.

We are much stronger and wiser than that. Now we can make a difference by bridging the gap, by simply taking responsibility for our words. Words are powerful; they are the vibration sent forth for good or ill. Through our words we can persuade others to see the way we see. Through our words we can hurt others. Through our words we can soothe and calm a childs fear.

Let us use our words to soothe and calm each other. Bonding as women is so very rewarding. Once the bond has been set in motion, and honest tools of communication agreed upon, there is nothing, we as women, can not achieve together.

Remember this simple rule: what ever words you utter towards or about another, the energy and intent behind your words will return to you threefold. We have the ability to perpetuate love or hate. It is our choice. The responsibility of choosing a direction is ours.

Unite with the sisterhood. Choose to make all your words an act of power aimed towards the betterment of this physical life and all relations.

PART THREE

MA-MA EARTH

The universe is full of
Magical things
Patiently waiting for our wits
To grow sharper[1]

...I had waited over a year to be invited to travel south to Mexico and visit a small cluster of islands off the Baja coastline. My friend, Kevin, was an adventurous surfer, and Toto Santos was just the surf spot to be the most adventurous with. However, I had constantly been informed Toto Santos was "for the guys only", and "too dangerous for females."

That never stopped me from wanting to go, though, and becoming upset when I was not invited. Inside I knew I would one day see this mystery island, and wasn't surprised when, finally, I was invited to go. Kevin couldn't find any of the guys to go with him one week-end, and surf fever was cursing through his veins. He succumbed, out of pure frustration, to asking me to travel with him. He needed at least one other person to help him handle the heavy, orange, rubber dingy in which he and two other surf buddies had each invested a $1,000.

Saturday, late morning, we threw a few belongings in our packs, grabbed some food, hooked up the boat trailer to his truck, and headed south. Yet, for the years worth of waiting, and the excitement I was feeling about finally going, an ominous feeling lingered over me. I was afraid. I forced those feelings away and turned to Kevin who was lost in his own thoughts while driving. I coerced him into chit chat.

Early afternoon we crossed the border into Tijuana and continued south towards Ensenada. Silence engulfed us as we drove the ragged highway, witnessing the ever-apparent poverty of the country. We drove past cardboard houses, half-completed construction sites, and piles of debris along the coast. Women walked with bundles on their heads as they returned home from the local market, and men stood in small groups around pits of fire where they burned their trash. Children ran barefoot through the dirt yards. And the ribs of the animals were sculptured on their sides.

Mexico has the quality of purity that California's Orange County, or any part of southern California for that matter lacks. The beauty of the coastline stretched on before us in its original state. There were no parking lots asphalted up to the shore, or giant condominium complexes crawling over the rolling hills. Bumper to bumper traffic was a rarity, if not virtually unknown. The ocean held different shades of blue within her depths, and the sky stood clear and bold overhead.

The rustic beauty somehow excused the level of poverty we considered the natives to live in, and in some mystical way the primitive spirit was inspired within me. I realized it was the land of unselfish, unadulterated life. Silent tears slid down my cheeks.

La Buffedero, a tiny fishing community, found us in the late afternoon just before the sunset. The sights of the village, still so primitive, resting along the powerful ocean coast was breathtaking. We walked along the thatched hut streets where the merchants prostituted their wares. Colored blankets, clothing, harachies, pinjatas, marble ashtrays and animals, wooden crosses, and jewelry spread out before us.

Free food was offered from the food merchants. "No good after today, must eat now. You can have for free," they yelled towards us as we walked along the cobble stone street. Shyly, I smiled, waving a refusal with my hand. Was I insulting them by refusing their generosity, I wondered to myself.

We followed the cobble stone street until it ended at a stone patio overlooking the ocean where two cliffs came together creating a V-shape. A roaring filled the air as the patio shook beneath our feet. We rushed to the edge of the patio wall and looked down to see the force of salt water as its crested waves crashed against the joining of the cliffs. The impact and the force of the saltwater thundered rushing up the sides of the cliff, cascading a ten foot high spray of white foam, throwing it back into the oncoming wave.

It was a magnificent display of power. The forces of nature were at work; two elements coming together. Each of the elements showcasing the individual strength and quality of their existence. I stood there mesmerized, unable to look away or think of anything other than the pure power that was before me.

Squeals of delight escaped my throat as the oncoming water gained momentum and the force of it hitting the cliffs lifted it five feet higher. The spray hit my face. I was acutely aware of the saltiness. Everywhere onlookers gathered. Broad grins and laughter broke out. We shared looks of unspoken delight.

We stood there, a mixture of nationalities, witnessing the water-show until the sun disappeared behind the cliff and an orange glow lit up the sky. I tore my eyes away from the cascading water and looked south to examine the curving land. La Buffedero was a community tucked into a beautiful, crescent bay. The southern point of the bay, unlike the power of the northern tip where I now stood, curved gracefully into a picturesque point. I imagined it to be a place were lovers went to picnic by the sea, or watch the sun set on their desire for each other. Beauty and strength. La Buffedaro was a place of natural beauty and strength.

My eyes followed the dirt road down into the main part of the community were the dwellers of this grace land lived. On the slopes of a green pastured hill a small boy ran with stick in hand. Ten cows lingered, grazing twelve feet ahead of him. He ran up to the first one and smacked the beast on the flanks waving his hands in the air. The air of familiarity swept over the beast as it slowly lifted its head, three times the girth of the child, and stopped chewing long enough to bellow a low, non-threatening "moo". Lethargically the black, spotted cow shifted its weight, picked up the first of its legs, and began treading in the direction the child was waving it in. The other cows followed in line. The child walked behind the herd stopping now and then to scoop a rock up in his tiny hand and fling it into the distance to see how far he could throw.

My child will never know the simplicity of this life, I thought, or the beauty of freedom this playground offers. I wondered why I thought of children. After all, my children were so far from being a reality, why bother comparing their life to the life of this child performing his everyday task?

I sighed, heavy with emotion and felt the touch of Kevin's hand on my arm. I turned to face his smile and sky blue eyes. "I'm hungry," he informed me as he encouraged me to turn and walk back down the cobble stone street towards the merchant huts which were now boarded up hiding the wares behind locks and wood. I felt like the beasts the child had so effortlessly guided, but willingly allowed Kevin to direct me.

We found ourselves sitting in an empty restaurant with bright lights and "rock `n roll" music screaming from the stereo speakers, vibrating from the loudness. The heavy smell of frying lard turned my stomach. I decided to nibble from Kevin's plate consisting of fish taco's, fish tostada, fish burrito, fish rice, fish beans, fish, fish, fish. I wasn't in the mood for fish and that was all they served.

The food was greasy, definitely tasting different from the Mexican food we eat in California. I washed it down with gulps of beer and instant coffee. Oh well this was authentic Mexican food and I might as well enjoy it.

The cold ocean mist began to seep through the open sliding doors bringing with it a familiar foreboding. My body numbed to the cold, my wild imagination took over. What in the hell was I afraid of? Kevin broke my reverie.

"Better use the bathroom here before we go," he informed me. I mumbled an agreement, gladly being distracted from the thoughts. When I returned to the dining room Kevin had paid for the food and was waiting outside by the truck.

We found an open field halfway into town, decided it would be the best place to sleep, and found a level spot. In the darkness we unloaded the back of the truck and rolled out the padding and sleeping bags. Not tired enough for sleep we sat in the cab, sheltered from the chilly, wet ocean air, and read books by flashlight.

As night wore on we snuggled beneath the down bags talking quietly for a while. A canopy of brilliant stars and quarter waning moon stretched overhead. Generators, which produced the electricity in the restaurant higher on the hill, eventually shut off for the night. Silence and total darkness coveted the entire community.

I lay there listening to the distant crashing of the waves, the soft snore of Kevin next to me. Shooting stars danced across the heavens. Slowly, the scene disappeared with sleep and dreams, dreams, dreams...

The rooster crowed as the first rays of light slid over the top of the mountains. Sleep and twilight faded as the scene of me driving in a car with a man who was telling me he had murdered the two lovers because he had to – it had been his destiny, just as I must do this because it was my destiny, echoed in my mind, shattering as the dreamtime slipped away with the night.

I sat up feeling the brisk morning air rush into the sleeping bag pushing the nights warmth out. A shiver ran through me. The cock crowed. I glanced at Kevin's sleeping form, then up to take in the surreal picture surrounding me.

Lush green grass covered the hills rolling down to the shore. A two lane blacktop road snaked through the community disappearing over the southern rim of the bay. Tiny, curling strands of smoke rose from metal tubes jutting out of the roofs of the shacks below. An occasional bellow from a cow broke the morning quiet, while soliciting a chorus of barking from a hidden dog.

The slamming of a door brought my attention to the first person to stir on this rose cast morning. An old man stood upon a porch, his hands slowly working the buttons of his worn blue plaid shirt through their holes. He snorted, spit, then disappeared around the corner of a shack.

Kevin sat up next to me. His blond curls matted. "Okay, let's get going." He spoke quietly as he crawled out from under the sleeping bag and struggled into the jeans he had kept rolled up beside his pillow. I glanced towards the steel, grey ocean. A blanket of fog hid any trace there might be on a clear morning of the island we were about to boat out to.

My stomach turned. Suddenly the images from my dream flashed before my eyes. "...I murdered the bitch and her lover because it was my destiny, just as you must do this because it is your destiny..." echoed in my mind. I wanted to go home, or shopping in the little town, or just hike around the countryside for the day. But I definitely did not want to go to the island.

We headed back on the road we came into town on. The sun slipped over the surrounding hills highlighting the purity of the land. The light was bright, the rays burning into my eyes, blinding me. The sky was suddenly fresh and blue and cloudless. It was picture perfect.

Kevin pulled the truck off onto a dirt road to the left. "There's this old fishing ramp down there," he confided in me as we bumped along the pothole road. "No one really knows about it. We used it once. Sure hope just you and me can get the boat off the truck and down the ramp without too much trouble. It took four of us last time." Oh great, I thought to myself.

"Well, at least we have hind wheels on the boat now, so we should be able to roll it on down the ramp." I managed to smile at him.

It was breathtaking actually, the little bay and cobble stone fishing ramp. The water lapped against the jetty and the shore. We were at a place where the land curved right displaying the Baja coast as it crawled north fading from sight. It was magnificent. The morning fog had almost burned off leaving a layer of mist above the land. Large ocean liners ten or so miles up the coast gave the only indication an actual merchant harbor existed, while breaking the illusion of being on a primitive land.

We came to a stop fifteen feet before the ramp. The dirt road slanted down at a sharp angle. Two vacant cars sat at opposite sides of the dirt field. A Chevy station wagon dented in several places exposing raw metal to the elements. Rust having accumulated along the exposed parts. It bore a Mexico license plate.

"Local fisherman," Kevin mumbled as he nodded towards the car. "But that one," indicating with his hand at a Bronco Charger and empty boat trailer hooked to the tailgate, "are more surfers. Which means," he grumbled. "Toto is going to be crowded."

Well, suddenly I was relieved – a little. Knowing that there would be other people out there held at bay some of the fright which was beginning to creep out from behind my eyes. "Oh, you mean there will be others out there with us?" I asked, trying to sound calm.

"There always is." He answered sounding disappointed. I felt enthusiastic. Maybe this fear was for nothing, I rationalized. May be it was leaping up in my mind because this was a new adventure and I was consciously aware that I was pitting myself against the mercy of the elements. Still, I could not quite shake the fear.

I packed a light lunch in Kevin's burnt, orange day pack while he made sure necessary items were in the boat. I pulled out my turquoise pack and unzipped it. I was going to be spending the day alone on a deserted island, and planned to do ceremony. The few items I brought for ceremony I carefully placed in the pack along with a bathing suit and towel in case I decided to sunbathe. By the time I was finished Kevin had prepared the boat and was ready to launch.

On either side of the trailer we stood, each grabbing hold of a thick, black rubber handle. "Okay," Kevin said to me over the top of the boat. "When I say 'go', start moving the boat back. Don't worry about lifting it, we are going to walk it off the trailer, okay?" His blue eyes flared in the morning light. I nodded, focussing my attention on the two black handles.

"Go." Slowly, the boat began to ease off the trailer until the hind wheels touched the ground. "Don't let go." Kevin panted from the other side of the boat. We continued to push the boat off until only the last three feet of the nose rested on the trailer.

"Use your muscle now. We have to carry this part of the boat down to the water, but rolling it on the hind wheels should make it easy." I nodded at him bracing myself for the lift. With relative ease we half-carried, half-rolled the boat down the eroding cobble stone ramp into the cold water. It sat there bobbing on the water inviting us in. A grin broke out on Kevin's face.

"Ships ahoy, Matey!" he said as his arm waved me into the boat. "Let's cast off." I climbed into the boat positioning myself towards the rear. Kevin gave the nose a final push then climbed in. We were off.

With little paddling the current of the water picked us up carrying the boat away from shore. The immediate concern was the sharp jetty rocks, but the tide was high and we were quickly floating in deeper water heading for the open bay. He pulled the engine cord, started the motor guiding the tiny craft beyond the small shore break a hundred yards out.

As he stopped the engine to unhook the hind wheels I was captured by the panoramic view now fully exposed. The little bay we just launched from was in the middle of a horseshoe curving in the land. The curve traveled south, the land rising until it towered above the ocean ending at a sharp point, a white lighthouse standing on top.

I realized the south side of the point was where the cascading water show of La Buffedero roared. Now I was excited. I wanted to get on our way. Despite all the fear, some instinct inside of me began to come alive. I knew this was going to be a special day.

Once the wheels were safely loaded in the boat, and the motor was purring softly, Kevin turned to me. "Are you ready?" He asked. I shook my head yes. "Hold on." He yelled above the roar of the engine as the boat jerked forward.

Blue met blue. Green met white foam. Seagulls danced overhead. The force of the boat moving forward at such a high speed slicked back my hair, making my eyes squint.

Exhilarated I managed to climb to the front of the boat where the nose lifted above the water. Air zoomed in my open mouth forcing me to close it. I turned to look at the landscape we were leaving behind. Beauty! The Baja coast lay shaded in blues and greys. The mist had risen higher crowning the tops of the rolling hills and cliffs. The land of enchantment. Life! This is life, I wanted to scream at the top of my lungs.

"Oh beauty of air and morning sunlight," I breathed as quiet as a sigh. "I invoke thee. You are a part of this moment. Everywhere your spirit dances. Be with me this day. Protect me this day. See that I safely return to the mainland this day!" I smiled into the rising sun, then turned my head in the direction we were headed. Closing my eyes I lifted my face to be caressed by the force of air as we passed through it.

"Oh beauty of fire. You are this land which dwells in the south. I invoke thee. Salamanders continue to play in the engine of this boat so we may arrive safely at our destination, and return to the mainland this day. Warm my skin. Let me feel your beauty live in my heart. Protect me this day!" I studied the coastline to the left. The coastline which would soon end and deliver us into the womb of the Mother.

As the coastline ended at its point my gaze continued into the vastness before us. There, as if magically placed, the tip of the island rose above the last layer of ocean mist. I glanced over my shoulder at Kevin.

"Toto Santos?" I managed to yell, pointing to the island. He nodded yes to my question, though it was obvious he had not heard it. "BEAUTIFUL!" I mouthed to him. He smiled.

Returning my gaze to the island I continued the invocations. Looking deep into the blue foaming water I continued. "Water of life, you lay stretched before me, beside me, behind me. Today I am riding the crest of your great body. This fear which still smolders in my heart is because of you. I know that I am at your mercy this day. Me, a mere mortal, challenging you to carry me safely from one stretch of land to another tiny patch. But I do trust you and honor you. I invoke you this day to help me overcome this fear. I know you protect me. I know I will return safely to the mainland. You are here with me now." I was not able to lift my eyes until the screeching of a gull overhead shattered the spell the Mother's womb had woven around me. A shudder ran through my body.

Pulling my jacket tighter around my neck I faced the north. The Baja coastline lay sprawled out like a beautiful woman sunning herself. Solidness. "Well, earth," I began. "It is your strength I invoke this day. The wisdom to understand what I must endure. I am of this land, I am supported and nurtured by this land. I will fear not. Protect me." I whispered to the mainland eight miles of ocean between us now. I would never make a sailor. I sighed.

"Mother of all life," the cloudless, blue sky rested above me. "We have lessons to learn in this life. I know that some of them are involved with fear. I love your body and would like to be standing upon it right now." I looked down at the endless depth of water. "Am I still?" I questioned out loud. "After all, this is part of your great planet. It is another form of you Mother, right? So what is the problem?" I paused not expecting a response. "I am opening to you. I am your child. Let your messages come through, I will receive them."

An involuntary laugh escaped my lips. I turned to Kevin and hooted. "This is wild!" I yelled. "Yep! he responded. I watched him for a moment, studying the strong jaw line which jutted out as he looked off to the side. His mass of curls now waves stretching back over his scalp. He had the sea worthy look. He must have been a sailor in his past lives, - many of them, I thought. He looked too comfortable, as if this was an every day occurrence.

He must have felt my staring for without looking at me he stuck his tongue out. I giggled and turned back to the island growing bigger.

"There are actually two islands out here." Kevin told me as he slowed the Zodiac down. There before us lay an island. "This is the largest one. It's about a mile in diameter. No one lives on it. There used to be donkeys on it. I don't think they're here any more." He continued to motor around the south point until we came within view of a smaller island a quarter mile further on. Pointing to it he said, "That's Toto Santos. The spot where we surf is on the northwest side. You can't see it from here."

There were two other boats anchored by the little island. A fishing boat and another Zodiac. "Let's go over and check out the waves. I was planning on leaving you here at the big island, but if the waves are no good I'll come back with you and we will go exploring." I nodded agreement.

We continued the short distance to the island then shut off the motor. Floating outside a small bay Kevin studied the waves. He explained that local fishermen could be hired to bring surfers out to the island, and that because of the fishing boats full of surfers, Toto was getting more and more crowded as each year passed.

The morning sun flashed golden rays above the cliffs which edged the small island. I studied the serene bay. The tiny beach rocky, no trace of sand. Tide was low and the shore waves gently flowed upon the beach. It was a deserted island. I wanted to spend the day on it rather than the larger one. I knew if I stood on the top I would be able to see for miles. As if having read my thoughts Kevin asked if I would rather stay on Toto. Without hesitation I answered yes.

As we motored closer to the shore it became apparent there were too many large, pointed rocks just under the water to get close enough to drop me off. I didn't like the idea of having to swim ashore so scanned the entire bay. A natural platform lay to the northern curve. The tide was low enough so that the six foot of rock stretching out flat from the others was exposed.

As we pulled within two feet of it we realized I would be able to jump onto it, but my departure needed to be planned according to the waves. The formation of the surrounding rocks would make it possible to climb to the rock shore. I gathered the items I would need and slung my pack over my right shoulder.

As we sat waiting for the set of waves to calm, Kevin planned the rest of the day. "I'll surf for a couple of hours, then come back, anchor the boat, and paddle ashore for lunch. I'll decide after lunch if I want to surf any more today, okay?" The plans sounded fine to me. We checked the waves and decided it would be now or wait another ten minutes.

Kevin edged the boat up to the rocks as close as he dare get. "Now remember, when you jump out of the boat push it with one of your feet away from the rock."

"Okay, okay." I grumbled back. I stood poised at the side, hands gripping the smooth, heavy rubber. My eyes were fixed on the platform rather than the oncoming waves. As the water receded, exposing the entire

face of the rock I jumped out of the boat and sighed once my foot touched the lava rock. Slipping and scrapping my shin against the next rock jutting up, I scrambled over the top of it in time to avoid the next wave as it washed over the rocks swallowing the platform from sight. It took me no time to cover the ten feet of rocks to shore. I did not turn to look at Kevin until my feet actually touched the shore of Toto Santos. And only then did I turn and wave.

I stood there watching him motor back out and join the other water-logged heads among the waves of this famous surf spot. I was relieved. I was on land once again. I closed my eyes for a moment allowing the fear to subside, then made my way along the beach to scramble up part of the cliff.

As my head rose above the rim I got my first peek of the island. A large smile broke out on my face. I was going to love this day. I pulled the rest of my body over the top and slowly stood turning round to take in the world that lay before me. Beauty! Everywhere I looked there was beauty!

"You will return a changed spirit." A voice rang through my center as the faded memory from the lesson's learned while approaching the island in the midst of my fear quietly dissolved in the wake of the beauty.

There were no trees on the island, only large succulent plants covering the ground. The island was very small. If I chose to walk the diameter of it, it would take only half an hour. To the north a large red and white lighthouse stood, the land below it slopping down to the beach which collected surfboards washed ashore from the grasping hands of the surfers out in the crashing waves. I squinted my eyes to see if I could make Kevin out in the water, but couldn't so turned to face the island.

I walked along a worn dirt trail that lead into a dirt road winding up the slanted earth to the lighthouse. Freedom rang out. I fancied I heard the lazy, lilting sound of oboes and Spanish guitars rising up with the ocean breeze. I was the character from the book Island of the Blue Dolphins. *I had a new world to discover. I wandered along the succulents to see if there were any herbs to identify, but instead discovered patches of abalone shells scattered everywhere. I was ecstatic, and collected the most colorful ones I could find. I made my way over to the edge of the cliff and looked down upon the bay where I had come ashore. Moving north I stood looking down upon the giant crashing waves and tiny black-dot surfers. I still couldn't make out which one was Kevin, so I sat down and watched the best and the worst of them.*

I was amazed I had willingly consented to ride sixteen miles out in the

*ocean to a small island in a rubber dingy. "I must be nuts," I told myself as
I felt the longing to do ceremony; the real pull behind coming to the island.
I needed to find the perfect spot. Rising, turning slowly in all directions, I
moved South. The coast stretching down toward the enchanted jungles of
south America. I wanted to receive information from this direction. I found
myself overlooking my bay.*

*Unzipping the pack I pulled out a beach towel and spread it out on top
of the succulents. I pulled out the pouch holding cornmeal, laid the pack
down on the towel, kicked off my shoes, stepped on the towel, and facing east
began sprinkling the cornmeal around the towel until a circle surrounded
me. I sat down and made a mound of cornmeal to set my large smokey quartz
crystal on. Beside it I placed one of the abalone shells I chose to use as a
censor for sage. I pulled out a red bundle which held a tiger's eye and power
feather. Carefully, I unwrapped the bundle. I placed the tiger's eye in my lap
and held the power feather up in my right hand. How it wanted to fly. Twice,
as I held it out in front of me, the wind caught the feather trying to jerk it free.*

*Closing my eyes I quieted my mind from all the wild thoughts urgently
waiting to live. My breath became focussed. The air, and the seagulls, and
the crashing waves against the rocks below joined the quiet rhythm of my
breathing. Warmth of the morning sun flickered over my skin, warming me.
The quality of this experience was altering what I considered my normal
state of mind; shifting it into a sense of non-realty. A feeling that was
indiscernible, one I had never felt before, came over me. I was at a loss for
words. For the first time I knew I would never be able to fully describe what
I was feeling. It was too great a connection with the life force of my
existence. I wanted to cry and laugh and throw my arms around everything
my eyes beheld, drawing it in close to my heart, hugging it to me forever. Yet,
I knew I must already hold it within, for it had become a part of my reality,
a reflection of my inner most thoughts manifested in the physical. Was this
what I truly thought raw life was all about? Was this Mother Earth?*

*Holding the hawk feather so boldly out in front of me, eyes shut tight,
I felt every aspect , every dimension, every possibility of life. The forces,
those unfathomable forces surrounding life flooded my being touching
every subtle body our physical ones are known to contain. I sparkled with
this essence. Breathed in and released this essence. The beating of my heart
pumped this essence through my veins.*

Something deep within my mind told me, that if I chose to, I could cease to exist in the manner of which I had been, and the possibility of actually rising into the very midst of this essence was being offered to me. I became giddy with this invitation and felt my spirit, my life force begin to gently rise. The roaring of the waves, the chatter of the seabirds, the beating of my heart echoed in my ears. The very taste of minerals from not only the salt water below me, but the soil upon which I sat, saturated my mouth. The fresh green succulents, lying smashed below, tantalized my nose. The rotting residue of abalone meat, left in the shells I had collected, was sharp and pungent. The exposed skin of my arms felt the coolness of the ocean's misty breeze, while the burning rays of the sun dried the cool, moisture almost immediately.

My senses had become acute. My vibration was at such a high rate that I was sensitive to everything. Dropping my head forward I lowered my hands to the towel and let the feather drop beside the crystal. As slowly as possible I opened my eyes, sparkling bits of gold danced on the water in the bay below. Naturally and comfortably, the black head of a seal popped out of the water. Its long whiskers twitching in the air.

I lit the smudge stick, scenting the circle. I sat there. Stillness. I surveyed the canvas before me. The rocky cliffs and shore below me. The southern portion of the large island floating brown and tan in the turquoise blue water. Far off in the distance the Baja coast, a white and fuzzy mirage rolling endlessly beyond my sight. The sky, the faintest shade of blue surrendering to white as it floated down to meet the land. The whole picture fading to white, an unfinished canvas. What did it need to look like? Or was I simply on a cloud?

A cloud that floated in the hazy recesses of my mind. My creation, my unfinished landscape of purity. Was this a remembrance of other times, other worlds? Too many questions racked my human brain. I lowered my eyes to the tiger's eye I held caressing in my hands.

Ah yes! Clarity of mind. The tiger's eye piercing through everything. The golden orange giving way to patterns of rich browns. I held it up to my forehead between my eyes. "Let your shaman's eye see." I heard in my mind. "Open, open, receive."

Flapping wings, seagulls screeched a warning to each other. "You are the hawk. Perceive you aggressor, you predator." Below me lay the island. I dove into a cluster of seagulls gathered on the cliffs. Noisily they scattered.

The morsels of meat in the abalone shells glistened in the sun. My powerful wings held me still long enough to pull the morsels free, then effortlessly carried me swiftly beyond the seagulls reach.

"You are the mother who must feed and protect. You are ruthless in that occupation. Great protectress of the children," echoed in the misty clouds swallowing the hawk as she rose higher. Sharply, the hawk eye flashed in my mind. Her screech shattering my eardrums jerked me back. For a moment, I forgot where I was and dropped the stone I held.

I glanced around, sweat rolling down my brow. I was visibly shaken, my body lightly trembling. I tasted bile in my mouth and a wave of nausea rolled through me. As I sat there in this state of confusion a vibrating voice rose from the earth flooding through me.

"Regain what was lost. Open to this power. All that you see is of use — the water as it meets earth becomes mist carried up onto the land by air, and is then absorbed into the land or evaporated by the heat of the sun's fire. But these are common things of knowledge, no?" No, I thought. These are things taken for granted. The roaring wave of vibration continued. "It is true, many have forgotten this common function, this common knowledge. Look around you." I did as I was instructed. "Everywhere, the power of nature stands strong reminding us of her strength — her power. All of this is the Mother. When you lift your eyes continually to the heavens you lose sight of this, and forget your connection to the earth, this your life, these your bones, this your foundation.

"You must bring their eyes out of the clouds and back to the earth. Help them see this truth once more. When will you learn this is where you are suppose to be, not in some make-believe concept of "heaven", but here on earth respecting and revering this great Mother body." I glanced up to the light blue sky above me. The cloud light which engulfed me on this mystical day. As if blowing by with the breeze off the ocean I heard, "Remember, it is not out there, but right here, right here, right here..."

I stood turning towards the surfers. As I did so I saw Kevin paddling on his board back to the boat. He was coming ashore. Carefully I packed away the items spread before me and made my way to the cliff above the bay. I sat down, my feet dangling over the ledge and watched as Kevin anchored the boat and paddled a shore. The slick, black head of the seal rose above the water between the boat and Kevin. First it watched Kevin moving towards shore, then turning to see the boat behind it a visible shudder ran through it, and quickly it slipped below the water.

We strolled over to the west side of the island and sat among the cactus and succulents to eat our lunch. We talked little, both absorbed in the unrealness of the day. Together we lay back and fell asleep on this island in the sea, under a turquoise sky, the call of the seabirds overhead. The sun warmed our bodies taking us deeper into oblivion. We woke in the early afternoon. Both sitting up at the same time, glancing around as if we had visitors. I hoped we would begin our journey back to the mainland before it got later, but Kevin decided to go back out for another hour. The fear sprang back. I knew this was the mistake I had been receiving.

I stood watching him climb down the cliff and paddle out to the boat. I began moving along the ledge towards the lighthouse watching him start the boat, motor it over to the other boats, and anchor. I sat down on the cliff overlooking the surfers and watched as Kevin mingled with them. I lay back, staring into the sky. Softly I slipped back into sleep. I must have slept for another hour. The sun woke me, or the feeling of being called by someone or something. I sat up looking around. There was no one near. Shading my eyes with my hand I tried to see which black figure was Kevin, thinking he might be looking for me, but again he was lost to my eyes.

Then I saw them. Traveling south. Hump-backed whales. Five of them rising and falling. Blowing their spouts of water, disappearing from sight to reappear a hundred yards further south. I jumped to my feet pointing to the whales glancing down to the surfers. "Whales!" I yelled excitedly. Then it dawned on me... the guys wouldn't be able to hear me. I had to contain my excitement and experience the wonder alone. Sitting, I sighed, watching the migration of the whales until I finally lost track of them, tiny white blurs of water.

When I returned my attention to the surfers, Kevin was climbing into the boat. I jumped up, grabbed the towel and pack, and headed over to the cliff. By the time I scrambled down to the beach and arrived to the rocks where I had come ashore Kevin was within shouting range.

The shore break had gotten hostile, the ten feet of rocks and platform gone. Instinctively I turned to the beach. The waves, now three to four feet high, crashed recklessly upon the rocks. "Damn!" I swore out loud. Getting off this island was going to be a bitch. I looked to Kevin who was staring at the shore. He met my gaze. "Looks like you'll have to swim out," he yelled. "I can't take the risk of puncturing the boat on the rocks. The waves are just too rough."

I stamped my foot on the ground. "I don't want to swim out there. What about the packs?" I screamed.

"You're going to have to swim out here. Look, I'll anchor and paddle in and get my pack, take it to the boat and come back and get your pack okay? Go back to the beach." I turned and made my way over to where he had pointed. After anchoring the boat he paddled ashore.

"God, Kevin! This water is freezing cold. You have a wetsuit. This isn't fair." Again I stamped my foot. He laughed.

"Kisma, just put on your swimming suit while I take my pack out and come back. You can paddle out on the board okay." I agreed, but without much enthusiasm.

I changed into the swimming suit, stuffed my clothes in my pack by the time Kevin had returned. "Put your tennis shoes on you'll need them to get past the rocks. They're pretty sharp," he warned me. I did as I was told, then slung my pack on my back. The water was cold and sent shivers through my body as I eased out waist deep. Grabbing the board from him I slid on my belly. Using all the force in my arms, I paddled out to the boat as fast as I could.

Once we were safely in the boat I pulled a sweatshirt over my head and groaned when he couldn't get the engine to start. Panic. My mind began reeling. Thoughts of being stranded out here shot through my brain. I felt frozen with fright watching the other two boats pull away from the island, and us. Just as I was ready to stand and wildly wave my arms over my head to flag them down, the engine kicked over. My breath collapsed out of my lungs, my shoulders sagged forward.

What a day, I sighed as Kevin drove us around the south shore. We passed between the two islands and came to the north shore of the big one. "There is this place I want to take you to Kisma on our way back. It's beautiful."

Beautiful it was. We drove through tall rock formations, archways into serene swimming pool channels which opened up into the most beautiful lagoon where two thirty-six foot schooners lay anchored. It was a movie set. We motored around the lagoon, then turned, at last, to face the ocean *passage which lay between the big island and the mainland.*

At full throttle we zoomed away from the movie set. The sun only an hour from setting. We had stayed longer then we should have, a race against time had begun. A mile out from the island Kevin slowed the boat. "I want to check something," he told me as he opened the gas cap on the tank peering down into it. As if on cue the engine sputtered and died.

How many times that day would I have to freeze-up with fear, I wanted to scream. I sat there rigid, not daring to ask what was wrong. Instead, I sat there, glanced up at the sun sitting an inch above the horizon, watched Kevin calmly screw the cap on, looked first at the mainland – still fifteen miles away, then back at the island only a mile behind. I heard Kevin say he would have to row back to the island, to the lagoon where the schooners lay. I heard him say that perhaps they would have a couple of gallons of gas to spare. Then I broke!

"Kevin," the tension in my voice obvious. "What do you mean we have to ROW back to the schooners to find out if they have a couple of gallons of GAS they can spare?" I didn't give him the opportunity to answer. "Do you mean to tell me we are OUT OF GAS?" I almost screamed at him. He mumbled "yes."

My arms spread out allowing my hands to grab opposite sides of the boat. I held myself in place. "How? How can we be out of GAS?" I asked Kevin through gritted teeth. "Didn't you check the gas level when we got gas for the truck in San Diego? When I asked you if we had a full tank of gas in the boat and to be sure we did?" He began rowing.

His eyes avoided mine. "I thought we had enough." He groaned as his body pushed and pulled the oars. Stay calm Kisma, stay clam, I heard myself say. You're both in this together. Think. Think. Time seemed endless as the boat slowly inched its way back to the island. Finally we were within sight of the schooners. Finally we were along side the first one. Luckily a man and woman came on deck to ask if we needed assistance. Luckily they had ONE gallon of gas they could spare.

I couldn't thank the couple enough, and couldn't wait to get out of there. As we headed once more towards the mainland I was struck with a horrible thought. I pounced on Kevin. "Kevin, will one gallon of gas get us back?" I asked praying the answer would be yes, but somehow knowing it would be ..."No," He responded. "We'll need closer to three."

Oh, God, Oh, God. The panic rose up again seizing my heart. The sun had sank below the horizon. An orange glow engulfed us. I turned to face the mainland. "Kevin," I timidly began. "Are there any lights on the mainland, or will it be only darkness once the sunlight disappears?"

"No lights."

I thought I had screamed, or at least it seemed I had. I frantically turned around in the boat to stare at him, my mouth wide open, eyes bulging. Then as if heaven sent, a large yacht appeared around the south point of the big island. I couldn't find the words so just pointed at the yacht. When my voice finally made sound I told Kevin they would have gas, we must go to them for some gas. I told him I did not want to run out of gas again. The feeling was too horrible, too helpless. I reminded him we were running out of light, we did not have a compass on the boat. Once darkness surrounded us how on earth were we going to find our way to the mainland, did he know how to navigate by the stars?

He understood the logic behind what I was saying and guided the boat over to the yacht. Three fat men, drinking beer and eating steak gladly gave us "all the gas you need", and a bottle of beer "to keep you warm."

With the tank full, the island shrinking in size behind us, I grimly turned to face the fading light as it altered the land before us. We flew across the miles of water. Anger filled my mind as I sat there thinking about the situation, how careless Kevin had been with the safety of our trip. I wanted to yell at him, but I needed to remain calm. After all everything had worked out. We were making good time back to the coast despite the decrease in light. Soon, if all went well, we would be standing on solid land; this day over.

Glancing back, the islands were no longer visible. Blankets of fog had swallowed them. There was no longer light from the sun. We were traveling in twilight. The water was black. The rising coastline to our right was charcoal grey. The sky was slate grey. It was hard to identify where we were, or how much further the cobblestone ramp was.

Fortunately Kevin eventually recognized the beginning of the horse-shoe curve where the small bay lay. He slowed the boat letting the engine idyll. We attached the hind wheels to the boat. The shore was still a hundred yards off, but close enough now to diminish the threat of being vulnerable and at the mercy of the ocean and the darkness of night. We wouldn't be lost at sea, or run out of gas. We were on the last leg of the journey.

The throttle reared, pulling the boat away from where we sat idling. The shore break was much bigger than it had been that morning. We would have to be careful and not let the boat turn the wrong way.

The boat jerked backwards. I was thrown against the nose. Kevin throttled the engine, but the hind wheels had caught on some rocks we couldn't see because of the darkness. We were stuck.

"Christ!" Kevin yelled above the roaring of the waves. "The wheels are stuck. We've hit a shallow spot." For the first time that day Kevin's voice was tinted with fear. Waves washed over the boat tossing and turning us so that one side was now facing the oncoming waves.

"We're going to tip over." Kevin yelled as he struggled over the boat into the water. I turned to yell at him as another wave washed over me filling my mouth with water. I gagged as salt water rushed down my throat. Coughing, struggling to catch my breath, I held onto the side. Oh my God.

The adrenaline in my body was pumping, my heart beating so hard it hurt. Somehow Kevin managed to turn the nose of the boat to face the waves. As the next wave hit he pulled down on the rope attached to the nose forcing it to hold ground.

"Unhook the wheels, Kisma." Without thinking I scrambled to the back where the engine was and stuck my hands over the side into the water. I felt around until I found the first bolt, then began turning it until it came away in my hand.

"I've got one." I yelled as the next wave washed over us this time taking Kevin with it. He had lost his footing on the slippery rocks. "Kevin!" I screamed. "Kevin, oh God, Kevin!" I panicked. Fear ripped through my heart. Kevin was going to drown. The boat was going to capsize and I would be tumbled to shore, battered to death against the rocks.

Gasping, his head resurfaced. I stood up in the boat. Somehow, within the clutches of chaos a noise from shore registered in my brain. "Help!" I screamed at the top of my lungs. "Help us!" Out of the darkness three voices rang out. "Where are you?" they called.

As if a switch had been turned on, Kevin's voice boomed across the bay. "Hey, we need help. Our boat is stuck on the rocks. The waves are going to turn us over." It seemed as if all motion stopped for a moment. The waves were poised above us. The boat no longer rocked. There was a sense of calmness. Though, the stillness lasted only an instant, in that instant three grey shapes were visibly moving in the water towards us.

Without further delay, Kevin and I turned our full attention on freeing the boat from the rocks. The second wheel was impossible to loosen. By the time the first man reached us my hands were raw and frozen. As the young man came to the back of the boat where I worked on the bolt the other two arrived. I glanced at the three of them realizing they had been out at Toto Santos in the other Zodiac.

Somehow, they managed to get the wheel free. Together, the three of them and Kevin, turned the boat around and swam it to shore. I inched my way to the nose and jumped out into the shallow water as soon as I could see the boat ramp. I ran, splashing through the water lapping against the cobblestones, and did not stop until I stood on solid ground. I stood there, unable to stop the shaking of my body.

Both wheels had been ruined, one completely ripped off. The five of us would have to haul the boat up the steep, fifteen foot ramp and onto the trailer another ten feet beyond. The boat was heavy.

With two on each side, and one at the nose, we very slowly moved the boat six inches at a time up the ramp. It was strenuous. My hand ached from hauling on the rough rope at the nose. My back ached as muscles I had never used burned with action. After, what seemed an eternity, the boat rested on the trailer.

I stood there shivering, exhausted. The dark of night totally consuming us, the ocean invisible. The pounding of the waves against the rocks the only indication it was still there. We thanked the surfers, offered to take them into Ensenada to buy them dinner. They declined. They too, were exhausted and needed to make their journey back to California.

Thank you's were called out again as we waved them good-bye, the red tail-lights of the Bronco disappearing out of sight.

I managed to struggle out of my wet clothes into dry ones. I sat in the cab of the truck, drunk with exhaustion. No energy left to help Kevin secure the boat on the trailer. All I wanted was to sit quietly.

My premonition had been a real one. I was indeed a changed spirit. As I sat there with my head thrown back against the front seat I knew that a great lesson had been learned.

The lesson consisted of details - helping other's in times of need. I knew we were stronger for having gone through the series of "emergencies," and that we had made it with the help of others. Our own dedication to achieving the end result of safety the underlining principle.

Kevin climbed in the cab, wearily sat down beside me. It was so hard to even smile, the effort amazing. But smile we did. And celebrate, we did, in Ensenada with a huge Mexican pizza and steaming mugs of hot chocolate.

We drove the five hours in silence. Each reflecting on our thoughts, the days experience. Feeling closer to each other for having experienced the trauma.

As the early morning light touched the sky awake, the warmth and comfort of our bed hugged us safely to sleep ending the day...

CHAPTER VI

THE SOURCE OF LIFE

The earth is a living, breathing, pulsating entity. And whether we experience this aliveness through an adventure, or through the gentle, caressing of one of Her aspects such as the air, Her voice is all around us. She constantly sings Her songs to us, instructing us, encouraging us, beckoning us to come back to Her awareness.

She is the great power of the physical body. From her we were made and to her we shall return. She has been with us from the beginning, and she will continue to be after the end. She is constant, and it is the cycle of Her seasons and all growing things which contain some noble truth that reinstates with religion, or myth, or language all aspects of life.[2]

Whatever goddess or god we choose to worship, it is the Great Mother Earth whom, in the end, receives our homage. For it is in the clutches of our mortality that we come to accept that after our death the shell, which housed our spirit, will be returned to the earth. In that moment of realization some minute recognition towards the Mother Earth as "death" is seen. It is from this recognition that a reverence to her is then established.

Yet she is not only the embodiment of death, but the reminder that all life waxes and wanes. She is an ongoing testament to the true power of life.

She is the unknown, invisible umbilical cord of life. Life of spirit. Life as energy. Life as ever changing.

She reminds us that we are all connected. That there is only one heart, one mind, one body, and that we are simply extensions of that oneness, which is of her. It is her great body that is the receptacle for the essence or spark of life to flow through, into every living thing upon it.

It is her great body that forms all the necessary shells for the manifestation of the Great Spirit to dwell within. And within the very center of this lesson on oneness, we are shown that the physical is merely a temporary metabasis; it is the spirit which is imperishable.

What it comes down to is one fundamental truth: the Great Mother is our teacher; the great master so many of us search for. And we, her physical children, have turned our backs on her. We seek the meaning of life in laboratories and on the frontiers of space. We seek the answers to our questions through the dogmas of man's limiting and ever-threatening religions. And we believe the truth will be found in the ever expanding consciousness of industrialization.

Isn't it funny how we look in all the wrong places?

Do we really believe that life is all about how intellectually superior we can become based on how wealthy we get, who own's the most stock, or who can blow up whom first? Greed, ruthlessness, politics, power, control, religion, material wealth; is that what it's about?

Rather, shouldn't we become intellectually superior for the truest since of community? For love and the perpetuation of life; for the sake of spirit evolution/the final goal: absolute perfection?

We are one heart, one mind, one body. Let us hearken to the voice of the Mother, and let us turn to her once again in adoration. She holds the great mysteries, the magical secrets, the fundamental truth.

Let us begin by acknowledging the earth as the Great Mother that she is, and seek to know her. Right now, where ever you are, stand up and go outside. Find some grass and kick off your shoes. Step onto the grass allowing your toes to wiggle down between the blades. Feel the coolness, the dampness of the earth. Close your eyes, visualize openings in the bottoms of your feet. Quiet your mind, your fear of being seen doing this. Focus on the heartbeat of the earth, while you are doing this allow the energy of the Mother to rise up, entering through these holes in the bottom of your feet.

There are many ways to get to know the Mother. Hugging a tree long enough to feel the pulsation of life flowing through it, then bringing it into your own body. Laying on top a boulder, feeling the solidness beneath you. Pressing you ear against it, listening, until, finally, a murmuring is heard.

Standing, arms thrown out from your sides while facing strong winds allowing them to hold you upright. Wading through cool, tingling streams, feeling the current pass through you instead of around you. Watching the flower as it boldly stands, a colored flag of beauty, a treaty of peace. Then feel its movement in the palm of your hand.

Yes, she is everywhere. The whispering leaves, the gushing water, the howling wind, the still desert in the noon-day sun. We must not forget her. We must remember her. Now is the time to seek her out, and in our own way commune with her. Defend her - no compromise.

Unless we do this, she will be destroyed, and with her all physical life. Spirits everywhere are standing up, crying out in pain; knowing that our greatest mistake, our greatest failure will be allowing the destruction of the Mother. With that destruction, if we allow it, all spirits of this world will be severed from the ultimate source of life, utterly destroyed. We will perish into total oblivion. Wiped from the existence of life. Non-existence. Nothingness.

The heartbeat is strong. Dum-dum-dum. On and on, unwilling to stop. The vibration radiates, embracing everything physical. It mesmerizes us, drawing us deep within its spell. Life-life-life, is spoken over and over, radiating up through our feet each time they touch the ground. Listen. Listen to it now. You can hear it.

MOTHER EARTH MEDITATION

It is important to awaken your senses to the Mother. We see bits and pieces of her everyday (trees, plants, flowers, far-off hills), yet we don't really see her. We smell her constantly (fresh grass blades after being mowed, roses in a vase, herbs growing in a garden), and still we don't pay any attention to these rich smells.

Everyday we taste the Mother when we eat of her abundance, and instead of acknowledging her for one second, we lapse into conversation with the co-workers from the office, say a prayer to a God, read the paper, or are too caught up in our thoughts to pay any attention.

134 An Act of Woman Power

We know when we physically feel her. In fact, we're getting use to the earthquakes that "rock `n roll" us. Some of us even hear her groans before she starts to move. Nevertheless, she is taken for granted. As consciously awakening women we need to reawaken to her, the Mother.

The Mother Earth Meditation is actually three parts of study: Awakening, Connecting, and Forgiving.

Awakening

Throughout our neighborhoods there are schools, parks, and semi-wildlife areas. Find one within walking distance. One which has grass. Begin taking weekly walks there. Just sit on the grass and take in the surroundings; acquainting yourself with the school yard (I will refer to it as the school yard as this is the neighborhood place of awakening I use.)

We all know of our six senses: sight, smell, hearing, taste, touch, and the ever illusive intuition. It is these senses which must be awakened, bringing them back to the awareness of life.

On a comfortable day in your school yard lay back on the grass. Stretch out so your body forms a natural pentagram (five pointed star). The pentagram has many meanings and is often used as the symbol for micro and macrocosms.[3]

In the reawakening of the senses the body lies upon the grass imitating the pentagram as a form of supplication; surrendering the senses over to the Mother; the greatest signature of willingness from the conscious mind.

The pentagram represents many cycles in this attitude. Starting with the left hand moving to left foot, right foot, right hand, top of head, and continuing; the cycles are:

1. Elements of nature: air, fire, water, earth, spirit
2. Seasons of nature: spring, summer, fall, winter, continuum
3. Senses of nature: smell, sight, taste, touch, hearing
4. Microcosm of nature: mental, emotional, physical, spiritual, oneness
5. Macrocosm of nature: Creation (universe), Holy Father (Sun), Holy Mother (Earth), Holy Child (life on earth), Great Spirit (original womb, Great Goddess, God, Life force, etc.)

As you lie there upon the grass close your eyes and just be. Relax your body. Relax your mind. Let go of your thoughts. Let your breath flow naturally. Open your senses one by one.

LISTEN . Listen to all the sounds around you. First you will hear the mechanical chatter: cars, airplanes, motor cycles, lawn mowers, television sets, radios. Hear them, then move on. Next you will hear the human noise: children's laughter, athletes running by, adults arguing, babies crying. Then come the animal sounds: dogs barking and birds chit chatting.

Your hearing is becoming finer and as you go beyond you will hear the wind whispering through the leaves; the squeaking of tree branches. The mashed grass around you springing back upright. And then, you will begin to hear the movement of the insects in the earth. If you follow this sound you will hear, very quietly, the steady vibration of the earth.

At first, you will shrug it off as an echoing of movement, but then as you listen and tune into the quiet, steady vibration it will join the rhythm of your own heartbeat.

FEEL. Feel what is around and touching your body. Sunrays washing over you. Wind ruffling your hair and clothing. Insects crawling on your skin. Grass scratching your arm. A strand of hair tickling your ear or nose. The clothing you wear.

As you become aware of everything you are feeling,and you cannot feel anything else, allow your focus of feeling to go down into the earth. Again, listen for the vibration, and once it joins your heartbeat, open and feel that vibration flowing up from the depths of the earth. Feel it as it rises out touching you. Let it flow through you joining the pumping of your heart.

Listen and feel this vibration, this heartbeat of the Mother. Embrace it. Become sensitive to it. When you are ready open your eyes and look up into the sky.

You have awakened two senses. It is important not to overload, and so, you may choose to rest. Do not think that you have to awaken all your senses in one day. Sometimes it is wise to move slowly, taking what you have learned and applying it to your everyday. Then return to work on the awakening of the balance of the senses another day.

Whether a week has passed, or ten minutes, you are in the school yard stretching out on the grass, assuming the pentagram position. Close your eyes, relax, breath, open, let go of the world around you. Listen through the different levels of sound until you hear the vibration. Feel through the different feelings until you feel the vibration.

SMELL. Smell the different scents. Gas and diesel fumes, food cooking, animal excretion, your body odors, the perfume you're wearing.

Then smell the trees, the plants, the grass, the soil. Allow your nostrils to flare, opening to pick up the scent of animals, or the faint saltiness the air molecules carry from the ocean.

Smell is one of our least used senses today. We have eliminated the use of it because we are afraid of smelling offensive odors. What we no longer realize is that many of our brain cells are awakened through our sense of smell. A large portion of the brain deals with this sense.

The sense of smell has developed in us from earliest times. We relied on it from "smelling out" food, to actually "smelling" danger. Incense is burned in ceremonies to awaken an attitude of devotion, placing us in to ecstasy while worshipping the deity of our choice.

In times past instead of eliminating odors, convincing our minds they did not exist, herbs and spices were used to please the nose. Tussy mussies (herbal bouquets) were worn on the lapel or carried in the hand to sniff when strong odors persisted. Bedding was freshened by strewing lavender buds on the mattress under the bedsheets.

Potpourri was blended and kept in bowls around the house, or spices thrown in water and boiled upon the stove; the steam secreting an intoxicating scent throughout the room.

Today, we deny natural odor and as a result we have developed chemicals which not only kill our body cells (some items such as deodorants have been linked to such incurable diseases as Alzheimer's Disease), but which unfortunately have stunted our sense of smell to a danger point of closing off part of our brain.

I am not instructing you not to wear deodorants, or clean your home; what I am suggesting is use natural products instead of chemical ones. There are many companies on the market today which offer natural products, from cleaning items to personal hygiene. Think about this: if you take a shower everyday like I do, why do you need to roll-on or spray a chemical under your arms or between your legs?

End statement: let us reawaken our sense of smell instead of hide from it.

Now it is time to *TASTE*. Open your eyes and roll onto your stomach. Pull a sprig of grass and stick it in your mouth. Chew on it. Feel how the taste buds go crazy and the saliva juices start to pour.

Walk around. Taste a eucalyptus leaf; just a tiny nibble, or the rose petal. A pinch of dirt never hurt anyone. If you know how to identify dandelion, then find the plant and chew on the leaf, take it home and steam it. Eat it.

Nasturtiums, pansies, juniper berries, taste them. Your taste buds will be in ecstasy. Munch on a raw carrot, or eat a head of lettuce like a piece of fruit. Devote a week to eating only raw fruits and vegetables. Go to a fresh produce ranch market (if there is one in your area, otherwise a regular grocery store will do), and buy some of the those exotic items you cannot pronounce and dine on them.

The point here is to simply treat your sense of taste to the basics. Such garbage passes through our mouth that our taste buds are numb, and we are not aware of the deficiency of natural enzymes we have due to the amount of processed foods many of us eat today. Because of this the taste buds are dormant.

SEE. Sight is the most over used sense. The sense that, in many ways, is ignored. This sense is a session all by itself. Return to the school yard, and sit down. Again, relax, open, breathe naturally. Hear the vibration, feel it. Smell the life around you, chew on a blade of grass. Now sit there, and see.

Let thoughts come and go. Do not drift off into thought allowing your vision to blur. Stay there, and be conscious of everything you see. See the sky, the formations of the clouds, the atmosphere. See the buildings surrounding the school yard, the patterns they make individually as well as together. Notice the colors and the age of the structures.

Let your eyes see the human beings around you. The personalities, the relationships. Note the individuality of each person; the way the child absentmindedly wipes the snot off his nose onto the back of his hand; the young girl brush the bangs out of her eyes; the young lover's hands clutched so tightly together.

Watch the animals as they move around you. See the colors of their body; the way they interact with others of their own kind as well as other animal species.

Look up into the branches of a tree. See the matrix of leaves. The movement of the branches as the wind rushes through. Watch the flower, the leaf, the blade of grass. Lay on your stomach and peer down between the blades of grass. See the world which exists there. Look at the grains of soil; the shininess of it. See how the insects busy themselves.

Examine a strand of your own hair, the back of your hand, the edge of the blouse you wear. See the detail, the very fibers of the woven material.

Then close your eyes. Rest for a minute or two. And when you open your eyes, look at everything around you and see the life essence. See the oneness. See the layers, the patterns. See that you are part of it. And most importantly, aside from all the physical layers of buildings, automobiles, fences; aside from the physical layers of animals and human beings, see the Mother Earth supporting these layers. See how it is her very body which is the foundation upon which all the other layers are built on.

The moment of realization, kiss the earth, and send forth a blessing to your true home.

The five senses have been awakened. It is up to you to continue to use them at home, at work, or at play. Hear what others are saying. Feel the vibration another person is emitting. Smell out the direction you should take in a situation. Taste the abundance of the Mother, and see the unity of all life living upon the foundation and support of the Mother. And suddenly, without having known it, the sixth sense of intuition has sprung to life, and you are using it every waking moment.

It is good when the senses have been awakened, for you begin to function as a whole human being instead of in a sluggish state. You are sharp and on top of situations, and most importantly you gain control of your life.

However, you must continually work on being grounded to the Mother. Ah, there is that word grounded. Everyone is talking about being grounded. What is being grounded, or the act of grounding? Why, it is the awakening of all your senses! It is hearing, feeling, smelling, tasting, seeing the connection to the earth.

Connecting

Connecting is learning to be here, on earth, in this body, at this moment; grounded to Ma-Ma Earth instead of out there in the clouds or the twilight zone. It is becoming aware of your immediate surroundings. Aware of your senses so you can fully function from moment to moment.

The awakening of the senses is the first step to the connection. The second step is learning how to consciously ground your energy/awareness.

By grounding I mean connecting to the support system which is the foundation of the physical; alias Mother Earth.

There are many grounding techniques to use: the roots, the base chakra, the feet, the palm of your hands, the solar plexus, and so on.

Each grounding technique begins with focussing on your breath, relaxing your mind, calming your body, and opening to the energy.

THE ROOTS: While either laying down or sitting up, visualize roots extending out from your body and pushing down through the floor of your house; down through the foundation of the house until they break past the top soil. Allow these roots to push down through the layers of humus and granite; spreading and moving down through the rich minerals. Reaching down, down, deep into the very molten core of the Mother. When your roots reach the core of the Mother allow these roots to plunge deep into the center.

With each breath draw up this rich energy of the Mother. Pull it up through the roots and let it enter your body. With each breath visualize the energy traveling through your blood vessels, through all your centers, saturating every inch of your body.

When this rich energy reaches the crown of your head allow it to circulate within you, feeding every cell, nourishing your body. Now as you exhale allow this processed energy to travel down your roots back into the core completing the connection.

THE BASE CHAKRA: In a sitting position focus your attention on your base chakra (pelvic area), and feel this center of your body open. Allow it to expand. Now visualize a golden beam of light leaving this center plunging deep into the earth until it hits the very core of the Mother. Allow this beam of light to sink into the center of the core.

With each breath draw up the supportive energy of the earth. Pull it up through the beam and let it enter your body through the base chakra. With each breath continue to pull this supportive energy up through each of the seven chakras until it reaches the crown. As the supportive energy reaches the crown visualize it pouring back down through your centers, down through the beam, and back into the core of the earth.

Continue to breathe, inhaling the energy up the beam to the crown, then exhaling it back down into the core. As the energy continues to circulate visualize your spine becoming a pillar of strength; the beam of light the connection.

THE FEET: In a standing position visualize your etheric or auric body expanding. As your etheric body expands visualize your etheric feet pushing down into the earth; stretching and reaching for the very center of the earth until they land upon the very core of the Mother's energy.

With your etheric feet sunk deep into the Mother, feel her energy rush up into your field, feeding not only the etheric outline, but entering and feeding your physical outline as well.

As you inhale pull the nurturing energy of the Mother up into your force field until you feel your body radiating with the power of her energy. Allow the feeling that your physical feet are sunk deep into the earth's core consume you. As you exhale visualize your feet shifting ever deeper into the nurturing energy of the Mother.

THE PALM OF YOUR HANDS: In a kneeling position place your palms down onto the ground. Very quietly breathe with your palms until you begin to feel your own heartbeat. As your palms become sensitive enough to feel your heartbeat, extend your focus deep into the Mother Earth, deep into the very heart of her and allow the vibration of her heartbeat to rise until you feel it tingling the palm of your hand.

As you continue to breathe visualize the vibration of the Mother's heartbeat entering your body through the right palm. Allow the vibration to travel up your right arm joining your heartbeat. When you exhale visualize the mingled vibration of the two heartbeats (yours and the Mother's) to travel down your left arm and out your left palm into the deep center of the Mother's heart thus completing the connection.

Continue breathing allowing the love of the Mother to enter your body and join with your spirit enhancing your sense: love.

THE SOLAR PLEXUS: Either sitting or standing visualize a deep, forest green cord of energy rising from the core of Ma-Ma Earth and entering your solar plexus. As it enters your solar plexus a golden light around your navel beings to shine.

When you inhale the magnificent healing vibration of the Ma-Ma enters your solar plexus immediately passing into the major organs of your body: heart, kidney, liver, gall bladder, brain, intestines. With each breath the deep, forest green vibration saturates those organs repairing damaged tissues and leeching out toxins.

As you exhale the residue of toxins travel out of your body through the cord and is deposited in the Ma-Ma's core where is it immediately purified and neutralized. As the healing takes place the umbilical cord of Ma-Ma Earth can infuse the same major organs with light. As this happens visualize the golden light around your navel spreading throughout the organs until the inside of your body is shining. As you exhale visualize the deep, forest green cord turning golden and watch the golden cord plunge into the Ma-Ma's core completing the connection.

Connecting to the earth is the first step towards really healing ourselves. For it gives us the awareness of true energy. The energy which is our functioning power in the physical. By plugging into this energy bank we feed off our natural foundation; we sensitize our awareness to the living forces around us; abundant healing energy is invoked; once again we connect with the opening between this dimension and the next, wherein the weighing of our spirit evolution is judged, determining whether we shall pass from this physical life into another or move on to other arenas of existence.

...I was in Escalante, Utah. It was a beautiful day. My traveling companion and I headed off on a dirt road towards an area called "hole in the rock". As we bumped along the red, dirt road we decided to take a side road which would end at a canyon, Wayne's Wash, and backpack in for five to ten miles.

The day was spent in awe as we walked the wash; orange and yellow-leafed cottonwoods glittering in the afternoon sun. The sides of the canyon loomed twenty feet above us worn smooth by the aeons of crashing water sweeping down through it; blood coursing through the vein. The cliffs deep red; exposed arteries.

I found my senses springing to life as I instinctively laid my face against the smoothness of red rock. My nostrils flaring at the pungent, decomposing plants floating in the ankle deep water I stood in; foaming with trimmings of brown algae. I wanted to sink my hands into the cliff feeling the coolness. I wanted to hear the audible breath and heartbeat which lay smothered somewhere below me. I wanted to taste the rawness of this ancient earth, and so licked the sides of the caressed rock; my face pressing against it. I felt home, for the first time in my life. Home among the canyons of the Utah land.

We made camp on a sandy ledge where the canyon opened up after passing through a ten foot doorway. A grove of autumn dressed cotton-woods crowded the north side of the canyon: a sandy ledge five feet above the wash stretching along the south side.

I spent the last portion of the afternoon alone; my companion having disappeared further down the canyon exploring for ruins. I decided to meditate with my Medicine Woman crystal I had brought, and then crawled on hands and knees to find beautiful rocks and treasures. When the explorer returned the sun was setting. We ate a light dinner, realized we couldn't light a fire as we had left the matches in the truck. So we crawled into our sleeping bags, which I laid out in a sacred circle, and snuggled down for an early nights sleep.

I lay in the bag looking up into the multitude of stars. I felt the presence of the Sky Beings surround me. They were everywhere. Their voices dripping through the light. I was very protected, they informed me. The humming and occasional trembling of the earth rose underneath me. I felt so very grounded. I slept.

A being took me by the hand. We rose in the darkness. Below me the canyon and small black dots on a sand bank diminished. We arrived at some type of school.

"You are a teacher now," the Sky Being told me. "Here are new students. Tell them of the connection." I was amazed. Now I had graduated to "teacher" on the astral, but no one had told me what to teach.

"The connection," echoed around me. "Yes", I sighed. I had been given a guide. I looked at the silvery faced auras looking at me, a more physical spirit shape.

"The starlight," I began, and suddenly a spinning galaxy of stars appeared between the student auras and me. "Is our light. Our essence. It is from this origin our spirits are born. Each star gives off a light, and that light sends forth a star seed. The star seed is a spirit. One of our spirits."

I continued to speak, answering the myriad questions the silvery mouths asked. I spoke of remaining open to receive the light, and that by being filled with the light consciously we become connected. Our spirit awakens and we become a whole being.

Then I told them, "Our roots, our bodies," instantly I was holding roots in my hands, the galaxy having long ago disappeared. "Our roots, our bodies are the Mother Earth." The class now stood on a mesa; red and brown patterned landscape stretching endlessly.

"These roots must be plunged deep into the Mother so our energy source never be depleted, but remain constant. Our bodies are nourished when this is completed. Our minds, our hearts are healed when this is completed. But it is not enough to plunge the roots deep into the core. You must take some of them and mash them to a pulp."

As if on cue a mortar and pestle appeared. I began mashing roots into a pulp. "Once the flesh and vascular tissue become one, you must hold them up to the heavens giving thanks to the Eternal One, the Creator - Greatest of all Spirits. With your own hands dig a hole in the Mother's body giving back the flesh. Cover it with earth so she will also be nourished.

"Now, you have completed the true connection of body. You have planted substance of your being to perpetuate physical life on earth. This is the connection. You must bring it to your conscious living and continue the connection there.

"Know this secret: on the Mother many refer to it as `grounding and centering`. Here we call it the Connection."

When all the props disappeared and the class was back in its original place I looked upon the silvery faced auras and saw that around their centers (the navel), there was a golden glow surrounded by a deep, forest green ring. Immediately, I knew, they had received; their own healing begun. I was pleased.

Again, a Sky Being stood next to me. Taking my hand it led me into the bluish-white corridor I have come to know as my Shaman's eye. "You have done well. You have wisdom, you are protected."

I opened my eyes and looked up to the stars. They had moved further west. I glanced over at the sleeping form of Kevin. Soon it would be daybreak. The water gurgled softly in the distant. The huge cliffs towered over me. I felt for the live stone I had found the day before as I crawled on the sand ledge. I sniffed the air for the scent of the young mugwort plant two feet away.

I was rested and could not go back to sleep. Rose light crept into the sky diminishing the dance of the stars. The shapes of cottonwood and aspen trees appeared. The canyon walls red as blood once again. Then, as I looked upon the wall to my left, the face of Mother Earth appeared. Twenty feet above me she towered. Deep were her eyes. For a moment she smiled, a light, knowing smile.

It was her turn now to gaze upon her daughter just as I had gazed upon *her. And in that soft, rose dawn I was filled with a blessing greater than any before. Quietly her face blended with the cliff as the white morning light of the sun slipped over the eastern canyon wall...*

Forgiving

We learn to forgive ourselves, as we have worked with earlier, but true forgiveness comes when we are washed clean by the forgiving hands of the Mother. When and where this happens, can never be determined for it is Her discretion. When it does happen you will know it, for suddenly you will be seized by the invisible hands and gently guided through a ceremony attended by the elements.

Dedication, towards making the effort of forgiving others as well as yourself, needs to be initiated. The conscious awareness of continually finding forgiveness must become part of your character. Your senses must be fully awakened and the connection to the earth completed. As your spirit begins to heal and your physical body fills with light, the Mother will feel your readiness and reach up to embrace you.

...It was the week-end of my thirtieth birthday. In celebration, Kevin was taking me to Kings Canyon. It was two days before my birthday. I felt this trip would be important, a milestone of sorts. I was excited, yet disappointed we were not at the Grand Canyon, the place I really felt we should be. Having already acted like a child, when hearing we would not be going there, I resigned myself, good naturedly (after an hour of silence), to the fact we were going to Kings Canyon instead. Nevertheless, I knew deep, down inside "something wonderful was about to happen."

On July second the sun rose, cooking us in the down sleeping bags where we lay in the back of the truck. We had spent the night in the farmlands of Tulare; a large waning moon floodlighting the night.

We rose with the sun and headed for Kings Canyon, another hour's worth of traveling. As we pulled to the side of the road to look down upon the canyon covered with Sequoia and Cedar trees the sun beat down promising a hot day. The Kings River was healthy as it flowed crashing along its path.

By ten that morning Kevin was itching to jump in the river and finally we found a beautiful spot. We proceeded down the embankment to the river. The power of the water rushing over the large boulders creating a wind which rustled through the brilliant green cottonwoods. I watched Kevin climb on the rocks, hanging dangerously close to the rushing water. Several times I caught my breath, sure that he would slip and disappear in the crashing foam, his mangled body to be found hundreds of yards down river. If I were to enjoy this moment, I knew, I would have to avert my attention from Kevin onto the beautiful scenery.

I crawled out onto a large boulder to watch the water dance. The warm sun kissed my face and arms. Sprays of water, as it rushed against the boulder, jumped up to touch me now and then. A huge smile crept over my face. I began chanting to the earth. All the elements rose up: the water dancing and roaring, the air whispering through the leaves of the cottonwoods, the earth solid and supporting, the fire kissing my skin.

"Come to the river of forgiveness," I heard the voice of the water spirit speak, opening my eyes and peering around to see if perhaps another person was speaking to me.

"Kisma," Kevin shouted above the roaring water. "Come into the water." He urged me as he lowered himself into a nook between two large boulders; the water placid, forming a two foot deep pool. I climbed over to where he was, feeling a little uncomfortable; one wrong move and into the hungry arms of the water you could slip. "It will make you come alive!" he shouted before disappearing beneath the water.

Edging over to the pool I washed the cold water over my legs and arms ignoring Kevin as he teased me, saying I was chicken, a big baby. I informed him it was very cold and then made up some foolish nonsense about water this cold being bad for a woman's ovaries. Silently I laughed after having said such nonsense. I was a chicken. I knew it, and he knew it.

"Why wasn't I as carefree as I use to be?" I wondered. "Is that what separates youth from age? In youth we throw momentary discomfort to the wind. While in age we shy away from any sense of freedom because discomfort may be attached to it?" I was mortified at this realization. Aggressively I jumped into the pool, the iciness shot through my nerves, making my muscles freeze. A hoot escaped my throat. I woke. Holding, the

sides of the rocks I lowered my full body down into the water.

Sitting up in the water I washed cupped handfuls over my head. Kevin climbed over the boulders disappearing from sight. With each handful I threw over my head, beads of water rolled off my back becoming crystallized. The sun caught in the water sparkled, flashing and blinding me. All motion stopped. I looked up to see a surreal clarity shift the landscape. It was alive. It was so strange. I felt transported. The sensation of being half-in, and half-out, but half-in and half-out of what? A swirling chorus of voices erupted.

"Let the water wash away aggression. Forgive. Let the forgiveness roll off your back taking with it all hostilities felt towards anyone. Forgiveness, forgiveness, forgiveness." Feathery hands stroked my skin. Water washed over me. I was free. Exhilarated. Laughter rang out of me. Smiles creased my lips. Peering down, the reflection of my face beamed up at me.

I threw water everywhere. "I forgive." I laughed at the top of my lungs. "I am forgiven." I splashed, lowering into the pool once more to be consumed, swallowed. I rose crystalline, sparkling. I climbed back to the boulder I first sat on and lay down on my belly.

The crashing water was silent. The air was silent. The earth was silent. The fire was silent. This made me look up; searching for the reason. The shadows on the bank across the river shimmered with movement. A glimpse here, something over there, yet nothing concrete, solid. Then it came. Musical voices.

"We are here." They sang. Sunlight glistened on the lurid water. Sparkling spirits dancing upon the surface. Power of emotion of the heart. Forceful. It could carry anything away, or swallow it; drowning its life away.

"We are here." They chimed. Air swirling through cottonwoods. Rolling on my back I looked up into the branches canopying over me. Shimmering leaves danced, whispering, whispering to me. The tree spirit formed. Leafy heads bowing down to me; bending lower and lower to gently caress my face.

"We are here." They kissed me. Fire embraced me. My body warming. The sensation of thousands of hands drying my skin, taking away the chill of the water. Caressing, caressing, smoothing away the residue of my former self. Exposing the new skin, the shiny, new skin.

"We are here." They breathed. Solidness beneath me. Throbbing heartbeat pulsing, poking my back. Constant vibration wafting through me. Shaking me, supporting me.

"I am here." Blue dress. White, fluffy hair. Everywhere she spread; endless. Embodying all within the circle of her arms. Allowing us to rest upon her body. "You are forgiven." Evaporating chimes. Purged.

I don't know how long I lay engrossed in the encounter. I was mesmerized beyond understanding. Taken out of time into a world not quite real. Yet, more substantial than the one I woke to everyday.

In time, my spirit quieted, the other world withdrew. I sat up blinking, glancing around, finding Kevin walking back towards were I was. Perhaps, it was his returning which broke the spell. Perhaps, it was just time for me to return. As I stood up to meet him I heard the faint whispering of a woman's voice, "We are one," before it was lost in the roaring laughter of the rushing water of the Kings River...

That experience showed me more in life than any other to date. I gained forgiveness, a true embracing of every aspect of living here on this planet. I like to think it was my birthday gift from nature; an acknowledgement that somewhere, somehow I really am doing the right thing.

Since that day I have been brought into contact with Native American ceremonies and learned a yearly ceremony performed in spring. It is a ceremony of renewal and forgiveness. A friendship ceremony.

After having been introduced to this particular ceremony, I realized I was being given the tool to use towards keeping my spirit purged, especially, after having been forgiven and cleansed by nature.

Though I have not had the personal experience of performing this ceremony annually as a preparation for the ceremony of the Mother, I have received confirmation that others can begin using this ceremony as a form of training in anticipation of the day when the Mother will come to you. I believe this to be true. After all, rehearsal has never hurt anyone.

Forgiveness Ceremony

The forgiveness ceremony should be done once a year, preferable in the spring. It can be done outside by water (ocean, river, lake, stream), or indoors (bowl of water, sink, bathtub). You can also visualize yourself by a great body of water.

Begin by offering a prayer of thanksgiving for the time of renewal, of forgiving. Take handfuls of water and throw them over your shoulder seven times in the act of "washing away" the residue of negative emotions, and of cleaning out the obstacles which prevent you from having positive relationships with certain people.

An affirmation should be spoken. One which states your desire as you wash away anger, doubt, mistrust, ignorance. As you let go of pain, sorrow, stubbornness. As you receive the light of renewal, of purging.

Allow your heart center to fill with the light of renewal and radiate outward, drawing into it the heart centers of those people with whom you are desiring to be in accord.

When you have finished, rise out of the water, dry yourself off with a towel. Begin a new affirmation, affirming the new relationships.

Send forth this new vibration by lighting a white candle allowing the rays to float the affirmation into the world around you, into the hearts of those you focus on.

End by giving thanks to the Mother.

CHAPTER VII

WOMEN AS CARETAKERS

The great revolving orb we call earth is a planet of female energy. It is a living planet, which means it continually perpetuates a cycle of life. This female energy rises off the surface encasing itself in an atmospheric womb which incubates the seeds, germinating them to grow.

Because the planet is living, all power upon the surface of it has the same source.

Those of us born into a female body have an advantage over those born into a male body. We are the same energy as our power source. We are born already understanding feminine consciousness. This makes us natural caretakers of life right from the beginning.

Men are born into this life seeking the woman, who is goddess to them. A goddess who is of the same energy as their power source. A goddess who will teach them how to live in balance upon the Mother.

Unfortunately, in society today we are experiencing a balance upset caused thousands of years ago. Men grow up being told it is a "man's world." Due to their natural tendency to turn towards a woman for caretaking, their ego/mind has had to undergo radical changes. Their egos have enlarged in order to accept this misunderstanding. Thus creating an aggressive energy which permeates the natural boundaries of nature.

Women grow up also being told it is a "man's world," and are taught to give their natural power away to men. Intuitively we know this to be a wrong. Therefore, we refuse to teach men how to live.

Mass confusion is the extreme result of the imbalance. No one know's what they really are. Senses shut down as a coping device against the natural tendencies and desires we have, which are continually being pointed out to us as being wrong. In the end, everyone gives away their power.

In search for a publisher of this book, I sent a letter of inquiry to a feminist publishing house, and received the following response:

`...I have many problems with the underlying assumptions and the political framework–both of which seem to lead to the conclusion that women are somehow intrinsically closer to nature and all of its attendant nurturing abilities. To me, the linking of women to "mother earth" and special caretaking abilities, etc. is a dangerous sort of biological reduction-ism that does not really challenge patriarchy's (mostly biologically based) definition of women. What it almost seems to do instead is accept the patriarchal definition of women as being linked to dark, mysterious, life-giving nature, but rather than disparaging these qualities, as patriarchy does, embraces and affirms and celebrates them. It is, of course, a positive understanding of women, but it does not do enough to challenge patriarchal assumptions...`

I thought a long time on what this woman had written. At the end of my musing, more than anything, I wanted to send her a copy of this book. I wanted to sit down and talk with her, work with her, help her understand the dilemma she was allowing herself to exist in. The dilemma of not taking her power as a woman. The dilemma of still giving her power away, even though, she thought she was liberated.

I would like to thank her now for that letter. It has given me the clarity on what it is I need to say next.

The quintessence of women being closer to nature, linked to Mother Earth through the same energy level, and outfitted with natural abilities at being a true caretaker lends no need toward challenging the patriarchy's definition of women, nor any desire to do so.

When we challenge the patriarchy, we do so out of our own self-delusions; our confusion of what it means to be a woman. If we work towards our natural essence, the female energy; if we embrace it and begin working from it we take back our power. We see clearly those attitudes which we must strive to invoke in others. We come to know that having a "stand-off" with the age-old and dying patriarchy is accepting the patriarchal definition of women, which reeks of submissiveness and inadequacy more than anything else.

A woman of power *is* dark as well as filled with light. She *is* mysterious, for she has found the completeness so many of us have lost and search for. She *is* life-giving and gladly affirms and celebrates this.

A woman who embraces her power knows that as a caretaker of life she holds the mysterious darkness, and is responsible for not only life, but death as well. The darkness which houses the understanding of knowing when it is right to be the conduit for birthing a new spirit into this world. The sense of knowing when she must not conceive, therefore, hindering the male sperm from traveling to join her seed. She also understands the necessity for sometimes aborting life.

A woman of power is fully awakened and desires to cultivate balance in her life and world-wide. She is aware of the shifting age, the need for bringing a semblance of natural order back to this physical life.

Now is the time to discard the hostile attitude the sexes have had towards each other for the last few millennia. Now is the time to let it go, come full circle to the true partnership of life.

It is *disparaging* to continue the date-less and ignorant posture of matriarchy -vs- patriarchy. We are better than that now. We are consciously awakening. The light is shining on the path of solidarity. Let's walk it together.

BECOMING A CARETAKER

When the late summer is passing and autumn is upon the land this ritual should be performed. This is an act of consecration.

On the first moon cycle during this season, on the day of your heaviest bleeding, spend the day alone. If possible retreat to a secluded spot outdoors; if not, then to your bedroom.

(At the first sign of this moon's bleeding do not wear tampons, use only pads. This way you will allow your blood to flow naturally from you. Make a muslin material pad and stuff it with cotton.)

On the day of your ritual have the muslin pad ready and go to your ritual spot. Do not wear undergarments, dress in a flowing skirt and loose fitting blouse.

Find a comfortable spot and sit on it placing the homemade pad between your legs. Allow yourself to tune into the life energies around you, opening all your senses. Tune into the Mother, joining heartbeats.

As you feel the first trickle of blood drop onto the pad, go into your center. Once there, become fully aware of your female energy. Allow yourself to surrender to meditation.

When you come out of meditation remove the pad, find a spot where you will bury it. Dig a hole and place the pad in it. Lay your hands on top of the pad digging your fingers into the earth around it. (If you cringe at the thought of touching your own blood you are not ready for this ritual. One day you will be. Take your awakening at your own pace.)

It is time to speak to the power source. It is time to "give-back" to the Mother part of you, affirming that you are the same energy. It is time to consecrate your being, and take back your power becoming a caretaker. Continue speaking until you receive acknowledgement that she has heard you and received. (Know that she may keep you there for a while.)

Once the acknowledgement has been given, place handfuls of earth over your blood. As you bury the pad affirm you are planting your life-blood, your energy, your power into the source of all power with which you are the same.

When the hole is filled place your hands over the fresh grave, open your heart. Search it. What is your true dream as woman? Stay as long as necessary to become clear on your desire.

Let the energy from your thoughts penetrate the earth. Visualize the energy pushing down through the blood, the pad, deep into the core of the Mother.

When you feel the energy sink deep into the core, pray. Really pray like you have never prayed before. When your voice is silent, give thanks.

Before leaving the area mark your new grave in some obscure manner. This is your power spot. You should frequent it. By sitting on this spot you will become that which you dreamed. Answers will flow into you. Wisdom will support you. Never give the location of your power spot away.

What does it mean to be a caretaker? To become the essence of the natural law contained within the skeleton of your physical body. To awaken your senses and remain connected. Forgiveness. And above all else, to teach, by example, the possibility of every living soul healing and finding wholeness.

MA-MA EARTH CEREMONY

In the spring after the rains have been and gone it is time to revisit your power spot to perform the Ma-Ma Earth Ceremony. This is a very simple ceremony, the concept being ages old.

Choose an herb, or flower that will grow in the environment of your power spot, and one that you are drawn to. Take with you seeds, or seedling of the plant to the power sport. When you first arrive sit upon the grave and meditate. Say a prayer of thanksgiving. If the soil permits, dig a hole with your hands in which you will plant the seed or seedling.

Into this hole place a fetish: a crystal, gem stone, charm bag, etc.; a symbol of your power. Break an egg into the hole, crumble the shell sprinkling the pieces around. This is the act of fertilizing the earth just as the sperm fertilizes the seed. Place your seed or seedling upon the fetish and broken egg.

As caretaker the act of planting seeds and giving life to a living thing re-affirms your power as life-giver. Should you be pregnant at this time, this is, of course, the greatest Ma-Ma Earth Ceremony you can perform. (If pregnant, instead of planting seed or seedling a cloth containing the mucus from your vagina should be planted.)

As you begin to fill in the hole with handfuls of dirt focus on the life energy and begin chanting "Ma-Ma".

When the hole is filled, place your hands on the fresh dirt (around the seedling if planted), and allow the chant to escalate, building with power, until it reaches a natural crescendo. Let go, allowing the vibration to flow down your arms into the earth where the energy will be absorbed and fed into the seed or seedling.

Affirm a blessing over the new plant. Pour water over the area in the act of nourishing it. End the ceremony by giving thanks to the Mother.

This ceremony can be performed every spring. In time, a magical garden will have grown around your power spot, or if annuals were planted you will be able to harvest at the end of their growing season.

By planting annually, even if it be one small item, we come to understand, in time, the cycle of life. The first few years performing this annual ceremony is easy to take for granted nature's cycle and even discard the ritual as easily as we throw garbage in a trash can.

With perseverance and dedication, a greater understanding is achieved, one that mere words in a book could in no way reveal to you. It is the end satisfaction of the harvest, the knowing, the being a part of the mysterious divinity of life.

Answers are revealed which are applicable to the relationship between male and female. New guide lines for teaching others are given. Stronger and stronger becomes your power. No longer are you just one of the other's walking around, living day to day oblivious to the basic laws; you become the basic laws. You become the purpose of life, the conduit of energy. You become a self-realized goddess.

...It was a day of omens, of goddesshood dedication. The wilderness was crisp and clean. It was the month of May. After hiking around in the brush we found a spot next to a dry spring bed. On the sandy beach we settled. A rocky cliff to the north, three quarters up the vine covered side a two inch coil of a snake peeked out of the crevice. Yes, this was to be our power spot.

We unloaded our supplies and set up circle. We changed into our ceremony gowns; blues, peaches, whites enhancing the greens and browns of the land. Grounding and centering we connected with the energy of the spot.

From objects of the earth we had been collecting; shells, dried miniature roses, clay beads, seed pods, bones, we began constructing goddess necklaces.

Singing songs of laughter we completed the necklaces holding them up to each other admiring their individual beauty. I took the necklaces from the women, then sent them off in opposite directions to commune with nature and receive their new names.

After they departed I sat up the altar, crystals and the new necklaces on the sand. I saged the circle and myself. I invoked the quarters, the goddess, then settled to meditate.

A short duration of time passed, I summoned the women back to circle using an instrument similar to the Australian aborigine's bull roarer, but mine being made out of plastic instead of wood and leather, which I had bought in a toy store.

The etheric sound interrupted the quiet wilderness. I continued to twirl it above my head until the women appeared; brightly colored currents peeking through the bushes. They stopped on the outskirts of the circle. Individually I purified them, then admitted them. Once inside we sat around the altar, smoked pipe, sending forth our prayers to the Great Spirit.

One by one we stood in the center, lit a candle while speaking forth our new names, Rabbit, Butterfly, Sophia; fertility, freedom, wisdom. Belief statements were spoken, the Charge of the Goddess recited, the "I Am" chant sung. As the dedication to our goddesshood reached a climax we were distracted by a loud rustling movement to the north of the circle.

All sound and movement stopped as we turned to behold the sight of two, three feet long diamond head rattle snakes stretched fully out not more than five feet from where we stood.

Stillness. The focus remained on this unbelievable sight. Finally, I spoke, "It appears we are being honored. They have been drawn to our energy and long to be a part of this ceremony." We looked at each other a little nervously.

"Well, how does everyone feel?" I asked. Butterfly spoke first, "Common sense says we should move, but I understand the sacredness. Even though I'm afraid, I'll stay." We all agreed a certain amount of fear had been conjured up by the mere presence of snakes, let alone poisonous ones. We agreed to stay and overcome any fears. We agreed by doing this we would be returning the honor this ancient symbol for "wisdom" was bestowing upon us.

"After all," I concluded. "It has been a day for omens."

No sooner had we agreed on the above, did the snakes eloquently slither off, disappearing under a fallen tree trunk with debris clumped around it.

As we drove out of the wilderness area towards the setting sun we each reflected on the day, the omens which had presented themselves, the two snakes. We felt powerful, truly goddesses.

My mind wandered to the Garden of Eden, the myth wherein the "evil" snake tempted Eve with knowledge; betraying god by giving the forbidden fruit to her mate; sudden awakening of consciousness.

I smiled at the irony in this myth and the experience of the day; the controversy surrounding the desire of Eve's for wisdom being the downfall and ruin of "man"kind. The words once read in a garden book, written by a Countess Von Arnim sprang to mind: '...had Eve a spade in Paradise and *known what to do with it, we should not have had all that bad business of the apple...'.*

Laughing out loud, I shrugged off the enquiring voices of the other women in the car. I played with the idea of the snakes coming to us in the same manner they had to Eve. Had Eve been celebrating her goddesshood that day in her garden? Had Adam happened upon her ceremony, witnessed the presence of the snakes, and in his own fear of these reptiles accused Eve of being evil?

No, goddesshood and wisdom was not evil, of that I was sure. So, was the snakes appearance simply the acknowledgement of the true nature of all women as that of our great ancestress Eve? That because of our natural caretaking abilities all forms of life have crept forward to her feet, our feet? And she, us, being awakened spirits feared none; instead welcoming them into the sphere of her/our world, her/our celebration of goddesshood?...

Yes, women are nature, the purest element of the Great Mother Earth. What an honor to be placed in the position of caretakers; of perpetuating life.

And so we gladly embrace the dark, mysterious, life-giving connection we are naturally linked to with all the glory of being attendants of nurturing. Proudly we affirm our power, our energy, the source of all power - Mother Earth. In celebration of womanhood, of goddesshood, we become healed; no longer just a part, but a whole.

"I am Nature, the universal Mother, mistress of all elements, primordial child of time, sovereign of all things spiritual, queen of the dead, queen also of the immortals, the single manifestation of all gods and goddesses that are. My nod governs the shining heights of Heaven, the wholesome sea breezes, the lamentable silences of the world below. Though I am worshiped in many aspects, known by countless names, and propitiated with all manner of different rites, yet the whole round earth venerates me."[4]

THE END

NOTES

PART ONE
WOMEN WHO BLEED FOR LIFE

[1]*Sister's of the Moon*, Kisma K. Stepanich, 1987
[2]*Witchcraft for Tomorrow*, Dorree Valiente, 1978, Page 157
[3]*Three Magic Words*, U.S. Anderson, 1954, Page 156
[4]*Special One*, anonymous

Chapter I - The Moon
[5]*Exploring the Cosmos*, Louis Berman/J.C. Evans, 1983, Page 23
[6]*Earth, Wind, Fire and Sea*, Native American
[7]*I Am*, Traditional Tibetan Chant revised

Chapter II - The Mensus
[8]*P.M.S. Conspiracy, The*, Felicity Artemis Flowers, 1986, Page 12
[9]*Woman Who Bleed for Life Ceremony*, Kisma K. Stepanich, 1988
[10]*Female Energy*, Kisma K. Stepanich, 1988
[11]*Woman Power*, Kisma K. Stepanich, 1988
[12]*Affirmation*, Gail Carr, 1988
[13]*Acceptance Chant*, Lisa Hill, 1988
[14]*Life Blood Chant*, Gail Carr, 1988

PART TWO
THE SISTERHOOD

[1]*Sister's of the Moon*, Kisma K. Stepanich, 1987
[2]*Moon, Moon*, Anne Kent Rush, 1976, page 376
[3]*Hertha*, Algernon Charles Swinburne

[4] WSR rendition of the *Lord's Prayer*

[5]*Positive Magic-Occult Self-help*, Marion Weinstein, 1978, page 209

[6]*Voices of our Ancestors-Cherokee teachings from the Wisdom Fire*, Dhyani Ywahoo, 1987, page 126

[7] Ywahoo, Dhyani, page 76

[8] Ywahoo, Dhyani, page 100

[9] Ywahoo, Dhyani, page 114

Chapter III - The Healing

[10]*The Woman's Bible*, Seattle Colition on Women and Religion, 1974, page viii

[11]Celtic Oral Tradition

[12]*God of the Witches*, Margaret Murray

[13]Statement from Women and Religion Task Force of the Church Council of Greater Seatle, accepted by the Board of Directors of the Church Council April 9, 1974.

[14]*Earth Chant*, Native American

[15]*Healing Chant*, Native American

Chapter IV - The Goddess

[16]*Bible*, King James

[17]*The Hero's Adventure*, Joseph Campbell, Video 1987

[18]*When God Was A Woman*, Merlin Stone, 1978, page 162

[19] Stone, Merlin, page 10

[20] Stone, Merlin, page 18

Chapter V - Bonding

[21]*Constructive Criticism-A Handbook*, Gracie Lyons

[22]Rhiannon, Circle of Aradia

PART THREE
MA-MA EARTH

[1]Eden Phillpotts

Chapter VI - The Source of Life
[2]*The Vampire Lestat*, Anne Rice, 1985, Page 409
[3]For several invaluable meditations on the Pentacle of the body refer to *The Spiral Dance*, Starhawk, 1979, Page 65

Chapter VII - Women As Caretakers
[4]*The Golden Ass*, Apuleius, second century A.D., as translated by Robert Grave

Author's Biography

Kisma K. Stepanich, who has spent many years worshipping Mother Earth (Gaia) and exploring the wilderness of Her great body, has now made available in the chapters of her first book, the feminine wisdoms gained through these many "bigger than life" experiences. Having worked with many Masters and Shamans of different traditions, and undergone several initiations into these mysteries, she tells us, *"The truest Master is Gaia, and the grandest initiation is when She speaks/moves/feels/sees/listens through you."*